The
Light
Between
Us

Laura Lynne Jackson is a high school English teacher and psychic medium who has been certified by the Windbridge Institute for Applied Research in Human Potential and the Forever Family Foundation. She lives on Long Island with her husband and their three children. This is her first book.

Look for Laura Lynne Jackson on Facebook
@lauralynjackson

The
Light
Between
Us

Stories from the afterlife.
Lessons for the living

LAURA LYNNE JACKSON

arrow books

3 5 7 9 10 8 6 4 2

Arrow Books
20 Vauxhall Bridge Road
London SW1V 2SA

Arrow Books is part of the Penguin Random House group of companies
whose addresses can be found at global.penguinrandomhouse.com

Penguin
Random House
UK

First published in the UK by Century in 2015
First published in paperback by Arrow Books in 2016

www.penguin.co.uk

A CIP catalogue record for this book is available from the British Library.

ISBN 9781784751067

Printed and bound by Clays Ltd, St Ives Plc

Penguin Random House is committed to a
sustainable future for our business, our readers
and our planet. This book is made from Forest
Stewardship Council® certified paper.

To my mother, Linda Osvald, who taught me to trust the light within myself and to honor the light between us all. Mom, any beauty in this world that comes through me is because of you; you are the root of it all.

And to Garrett, Ashley, Hayden, and Juliet, who have filled my world with light, joy, and meaning; you are my reason for everything.

And to all of you reading this—may we light the way for one another, always.

There are only two ways to live your life.
One is as though nothing is a miracle.
The other is as though everything is.

CONTENTS

PART THREE

INTRODUCTION

I WAS ON JERICHO TURNPIKE, heading west, when the messages started coming in.

I squeezed the wheel of my Honda Pilot and swerved right, pulling into a Staples parking lot. I hit the brakes and came to a stop halfway into a spot.

I wasn't ready for them. Just a bit earlier I'd been taking deep breaths, trying to stay calm, because I was so nervous. Scared to death, really. Soon I would be in a room filled with suffering people. My role that evening was to try to ease their pain. My fear was that I would make it worse.

I was wearing a plain black shirt and black pants. I didn't want anyone to be distracted by patterns on my shirt or flowers on my dress. I'd skipped dinner, because I was too anxious to eat. My husband, Garrett, wasn't home from work yet, so I'd asked my mother to watch our two young children until he got back. I was running late and I tried to make up some time on the busy road, but traffic was slow.

Then, suddenly, they started to come to me.

The children.

All at once, as a group, they were there. It was astonishing. It was like being alone in a room when suddenly the door opens and ten or fifteen people come in. You might not even see them or hear them, but still you know they're there—you can *feel* them. You know you're not alone anymore. That is what it felt like in my Honda Pilot—I knew I wasn't alone.

Then came the words and names and stories and pleas and descriptions and images and all the things they wanted to share, so many I had to slow them down.

"Wait a second, wait a second," I said aloud as I fumbled in my purse for my little red notepad and pen. I started writing as fast as I could, but I couldn't keep up with all the messages I was getting. It was all just pouring out.

Tell them I am still here, one said.

Tell them I am still part of their lives, said another.

Tell them, "I love you and I see everything that goes on."

Please don't cry for me. I'm okay.

I am not dead. I am still your child.

Don't think of me as gone. I am not gone.

Please tell them I'm not gone!

I sat in my crookedly parked car outside Staples and kept scribbling—a woman surrounded by children no one else could see.

Finally, after a few minutes, I tucked the notes in my purse, got back on the road, and drove as fast as I could to the Huntington Hilton on Broad Hollow Road. I raced through the hotel lobby and found the conference room where the event was being held. A sign outside gave only a hint of what would happen that night. It read, "How to Listen When Your Children Speak."

The conference room was ordinary—brown curtains, overhead lights, plush carpet, swivel chairs. In the middle of the room there was a large rectangular table with nineteen people seated stiffly around it. When I walked in they all turned toward me and fell completely silent. Their faces were sad and haunted. It felt like a full minute before anyone so much as breathed.

These were the parents.

The evening's hosts, Phran and Bob Ginsberg—the directors of the Forever Family Foundation—came over and broke the tension. They hugged me hello and offered me a chair. I said no thanks—there was no way I could sit, I was way too nervous. Bob stood in front of the room and cleared his throat.

"This is Laura Lynne Jackson," he said in a soft voice. "She's a Certified Medium with the Forever Family Foundation, and she's here tonight to help us learn how to talk to our children."

Bob stepped aside and gave the floor to me. I took a deep breath and looked down at the scribbled notes in my hand. The parents stared at me, waiting. I didn't know what to say or how to start. Another long moment passed, the thick, heavy silence returning.

No one knew what was coming next, least of all me.

Finally I just looked up and spoke.

"Your children are here," I blurted out. "And there is something they want you to know."

My name is Laura Lynne Jackson, and I am a wife, a mother, and a high school English teacher.

I am also a psychic medium.

I'm probably not what most people think of when they think of psychic mediums. I don't read tea leaves or tarot cards, and I don't work out of a storefront. I'm not a fortune-teller and I don't own a crystal ball (well, okay, I do have a tiny decorative one, but only because I couldn't resist buying it when I saw it in a store). I am simply someone who possesses a gift that is more focused in me than in others.

I am clairvoyant, which means I have the ability to gather information about people and events through means other than my five senses. I'm also clairaudient—I can perceive sounds through means other than my ears—and clairsentient, which allows me to feel things through nonhuman means.

I can, for instance, sit at a table in a restaurant and feel the distinct energy of the people who were there before me, as if they'd left dozens of bristling energy fingerprints. And if that energy strikes me in a negative way, I'll politely tell the hostess I'd rather sit somewhere else or, if it's the last open table, that I have to leave. Which doesn't always thrill my husband and kids. Or the hostess, for that matter.

Beyond my abilities as a psychic, I am also a medium, which means I am capable of communicating with people who have passed from this earth.

If your first question is how I got to be this way, my first answer is, I don't know. I've spent a lifetime trying to figure it out.

In my quest to find answers, I've undergone rigorous tests—first with the Forever Family Foundation, a nonprofit, science-based group that helps people in grief, and then with the Windbridge Institute for Applied Research in Human Potential in Arizona. At Windbridge, I passed an eight-step, quintuple-blind screening administered by scientists to become one of only a small group of Certified Research Mediums.

And yet, even as I was searching for answers—searching for my true purpose—I was also carefully hiding my abilities from the rest of the world. I didn't know where or how my abilities would fit into my life yet. I didn't know what I was supposed to do with them. For much of my life, I tried to carve a path for myself that did not involve being a psychic medium.

In my senior year of college I studied abroad at Oxford, and studied Shakespeare, determined to immerse myself in scholarship. After graduating I considered becoming a lawyer and was accepted into two top law schools, but I decided to follow my passion to teach. For the longest time I thought of myself as a teacher, first and foremost. Aura readings and spirit communications didn't have a place in my academic life.

And so, for nearly twenty years, I led a secret double life.

By day I taught teenagers *Macbeth* and *The Grapes of Wrath*, but at night, while my husband watched the kids downstairs, I was upstairs in my bedroom having private phone conversations with celebrities and athletes and astronauts and politicians and CEOs and all kinds of people, giving them a glimpse of something beyond the accepted bounds of human experience.

But here is the remarkable thing I discovered in the course of leading that double life—I realized that I am not really that different. Though my abilities made me feel that I wasn't like other people, that I wasn't "normal," I came to see that being "gifted" in this way was not the gift itself.

The beautiful gift I've been given—the awareness that we are all connected by powerful cords of light and love, both here on earth and beyond—is a gift that belongs to us all.

===

Like my life, this book is a voyage from darkness to light. It tells the story of the journey I took toward understanding my true purpose and the ways we are connected to the world around us. What I hope most of all is that you find something in my journey that resonates in *your* life.

Because if you do, you might come to the same understanding that I did—that the powerful bonds that connect us to our loved ones here and in the afterlife can, if we open our hearts and minds to them, immeasurably enhance the way we live and love today.

But even after I came to that understanding, I never thought to share it with the world. I had no plans to write a book. Then, one day at the high school where I teach, while I was on hall duty,

I felt a sudden, immense download of information and insight from the universe. It felt like a lightning bolt that brought instant clarity. And the basic instruction was simple.

You are meant to share your story.

This had nothing to do with me; it had everything to do with the message. The life lessons that emerged from the readings I gave were not meant to be kept secret. They were meant to go out into the world.

I don't consider this book a memoir of my life, but I see my story as a means to share some of the most powerful and profound readings I have done over the years. Readings that connected people with their loved ones on the Other Side and, in the process, helped them heal old wounds, overcome their past, reimagine their lives, and finally understand their true path and purpose in this world. These readings were immensely poignant and informative for me.

The readings, as well as my life story, are really all about the same thing—humanity's brave, relentless quest for answers. As a student of literature, I was encouraged to engage with the most profound questions of all: Why are we here? What does it mean to exist? What is our purpose in this life? I don't claim to have discovered all the answers to these questions. All I can do is tell my story. And I can share my belief that if we don't at least consider the possibility of an afterlife—if we don't look at the wealth of evidence that has surfaced in recent years about the endurance of consciousness—we are shutting ourselves off from a source of great beauty, comfort, healing, and love. But if we are open to having this conversation, we might become brighter, happier, more authentic people. Closer to our truth. Closer to our real selves. The very best version of who we are. The version that allows us to share our best selves with others, and in this way change the world.

That is all I want to do—have the conversation. I want to open up the possibility that there is more than just our traditional way of looking at the world. I want to explore what I've seen time and again in my readings—that the universe operates on a principle of synchronicity, an unseen force that connects events and invests everything we do with meaning.

I want you to understand that this very book has found its way into your hands for a reason.

Most of all, I want to discuss an amazing truth that has become apparent to me through my work—that brilliant cords of light energy connect all of us here on earth and connect us further to our loved ones who have passed.

I can see these cords of light. I can see the light between us.

And because the light is there, binding us, intertwining our fates, because we all draw power from the same energy source, we know something else to be true.

Nobody lives a small life.

No one is forgotten by the universe.

All of us can greatly brighten the world.

It's just that some of us haven't yet recognized how powerful we are.

―――――

I don't expect my ideas to be accepted without resistance. I've been a teacher for nearly two decades and I'm not easily persuaded by half-baked theories or moon-eyed arguments. I have always taught my students to be critical thinkers—to probe and analyze and question—and that is how I've approached my gift. I've had my abilities tested by scientists and researchers. I've spoken with brave explorers and profound intellects. I've followed the scientific developments of the last quarter century that have given us astonishing new insights into human capacity.

I've come to understand how the many remarkable occurrences in my life are consistent with, and explainable by, what we are just now learning about the power and endurance of human consciousness.

Even so, the most important lessons in this book do not come from scientists or researchers or explorers. And they certainly don't come from me. I am not a prophet or an oracle. All I am is a conduit.

The most important lessons come from teams of light beings reaching out to us from across the divide.

As a psychic medium, I have read for hundreds of people, some of them rich and famous, most of them not. In those readings I have connected them to their loved ones who are no longer on this earth. These loved ones who have passed offer us a miraculous view of existence and the universe.

The very first step of our journey is easy—it merely requires us to open our minds to the possibility that there is more to existence than what can easily be grasped by our five senses.

The vast majority of us do this already. Most of us believe in a higher power, whatever name we use to describe it. I refer to this higher power as the universe. Others call it God. I was raised to believe in God and I still do, but to me all religions are like a great big plate that's been broken into many pieces. All the pieces are different, but they're all still part of the same plate. The words we use to describe our beliefs aren't as important as the beliefs themselves.

And so we are already willing to believe in something bigger than ourselves—something we can't prove or explain or even fully comprehend. We are not afraid to take that leap. But if we take the *next* leap—the belief that our consciousness doesn't end with death but endures in a much greater journey—then something truly incredible happens.

Because if we can believe in an afterlife, we then must allow for the possibility that we can connect to it.

To be honest, if the astonishing things that happened in my life hadn't happened to me, I'm not sure I'd believe they were possible. But they did happen to me, so I know they're not just possible—I know they are real.

And I know that when we open our minds to the ways in which we're all entangled—a part of the same whole, encompassing past, present, and future—we begin to see connections and meaning and light where before all we saw was darkness.

PART ONE

1

Pop Pop

ON A SUNNY WEDNESDAY AFTERNOON in August, when I was eleven years old, my sister, my brother, and I were splashing around in the three-foot-deep aboveground swimming pool in the backyard of our home on Long Island. There were only a handful of days left before the start of school, and we were trying to squeeze every last ounce of fun out of the summer. My mother came out to say she was going to see our grandparents in their home in Roslyn, about a fifty-minute drive away. For years I'd gone with her on trips to see my grandparents, and I'd always loved going. But as I got older other activities got in the way, so sometimes my mother would go by herself and leave us behind. On this beautiful summer day she knew she had no hope of getting any of us out of the pool.

"You kids have fun," she called out to us. "I'll be back in a few hours." And that should have been that.

But then, all of a sudden, I panicked.

I felt it deep in my bones. Sheer, inexplicable, ice-cold panic. I shot straight up in the pool and screamed out to my mother.

"Wait!" I yelled. "I have to come with you!"

My mother laughed. "It's okay, stay," she said. "Enjoy yourself, it's a beautiful day."

But I was already paddling furiously to the edge of the pool, my brother and sister watching and wondering what was wrong with me.

"No!" I hollered. "I want to come with you! Please, please wait for me."

"Laura, it's okay. . . ."

"No, Mom, I have to come with you!"

My mother stopped laughing. "All right, calm down," she said. "Come inside, get changed, I'll wait."

I ran inside dripping wet, threw on some clothes, dashed back out, and got in the car still half drenched, still utterly panicked. One hour later we pulled into my grandparents' driveway, and I saw my grandfather—whom I called Pop Pop—waving at us from the back porch. Only then, when I got to see him and hug him, did the panic subside. I spent the next few hours on the porch with Pop Pop, talking, laughing, singing, and telling jokes. When it was time to go I gave him a kiss and a hug and I told him, "I love you."

I never saw him alive again.

I didn't know Pop Pop had been feeling weak and tired. The grown-ups would never tell me something like that. When I was with him that day he was his usual self—warm, funny, playful. He must have summoned all his strength to appear healthy to me. Three days after my visit, Pop Pop went to see his doctor. The doctor gave him the devastating news that he had leukemia.

Three weeks later, Pop Pop was gone.

When my mother sat my sister, my brother, and me on the couch and gently told us Pop Pop had passed, I felt a blitz of emotions. Shock. Confusion. Disbelief. Anger. Profound sadness. A deep, dreadful feeling of already missing him.

Worst of all, I felt a terrible, shattering sense of guilt.

The instant I learned my grandfather was gone, I understood precisely why I'd been in such a panic to see him. I had known he was going to die.

Of course, I couldn't have really *known*. I didn't even know he was sick. And yet, somehow, I did know it. Why else would I have demanded to see him?

But if I did know it, why hadn't I articulated it—to Pop Pop, to my mother, or even to myself? I hadn't had a clear thought or even an inkling that anything was wrong with my grandfather, and I hadn't gone to visit him with any kind of understanding that it would be the last time I'd see him. All I had was a mysterious sense of knowing. I didn't understand it at all, but it made me feel horribly uncomfortable, as if I were somehow complicit in Pop Pop's passing. I felt like I had some connection to the cruel forces that had claimed his life, and that made me feel unimaginably guilty.

I started to think something must be seriously wrong with me. I'd never encountered anyone who could sense when someone was going to die, and now that it had happened to me, I couldn't even begin to understand it. All I understood was that it was a horrible thing to know. I became convinced I wasn't normal; I was cursed.

One week later, I had a dream.

In the dream I was all grown up and I was an actress. I was living in Australia. I was wearing a long, colorful, nineteenth-century dress, and I felt beautiful. All of a sudden I felt a staggering concern for my family—the same family I had in real life. In the dream I felt my chest seize and I collapsed to the floor. I was aware I was dying.

Yet I didn't wake up—the dream kept going. I felt myself leave my physical body and become a free-floating consciousness, capable of observing everything around me. I saw my family gathered together around my body in the room where I'd fallen, all of them weeping. I was so upset to see them in such pain that I tried to call out to them. "Don't worry, I am alive! Death doesn't exist!" I said. But it was no use, because I didn't have a voice anymore—they just couldn't hear me. All I could do was project my thoughts to them. And then I began to drift away from them, like a helium balloon that someone let go of, and I floated way, way above them, into a darkness—a dense, peaceful darkness with beautiful, twinkling lights all around. I felt a strong feeling of calm and contentment wash over me.

And precisely at that moment, I saw an incredible sight.

I saw Pop Pop.

He was there, in the space just ahead of me, though not in his physical body but rather in spirit—a spirit that was beautifully, undeniably, entirely his. My consciousness instantly recognized his consciousness. He was a point of light, like a bright star in the dark night sky, but the light was powerful and magnetic, drawing me toward it, filling me with love. It was as if I was seeing Pop Pop's true self—not his earthly body, but rather this greater, inner light that was truly him. I was seeing his soul energy. I understood that Pop Pop was safe, and that he was in a beautiful place filled with love. I understood he was home, and in that instant I also understood that this was the place that we all come from, the place we all belong. He had returned to the place he'd come from.

Realizing that this was Pop Pop and that he still existed in some way, I felt less sad. I felt great love, great comfort, and, in that moment of recognition, great happiness. And just before I was drawn all the way home with Pop Pop, I felt something closing around me and pulling me back.

Then I woke up.

I sat up in bed. My face was wet. I was crying. But I wasn't sad. These were tears of joy. I was crying because I'd gotten to see Pop Pop!

I lay in bed and cried for a long time. I had been shown that dying doesn't mean losing the people we love. I knew that Pop Pop was still present in my life. I was so thankful for my dream.

It was only years later—many years—that I gathered enough experience to understand what Pop Pop's passing and the events surrounding it signified in my life.

What I had sensed in that swimming pool was the beginning of the voyage of Pop Pop's soul to some other place. Because I loved him so much—because I was connected to him in such a powerful way—my soul could sense that his soul was about to go on a journey. And sensing that wasn't a curse at all. It allowed me to spend that one, last magical afternoon with Pop Pop. If that wasn't a gift, what is?

And the dream?

The dream convinced me of one thing—that Pop Pop wasn't gone. He was just someplace else. But where? Where, exactly, was he?

I couldn't answer that when I was eleven. But over time, I came to realize Pop Pop was on the Other Side

What do I mean by the Other Side?

I have this simple analogy to explain it. Think of your body as a car—new at first, then older, then really old. What happens to cars when they get really old? They get discarded.

But we, the humans, are not discarded with the cars. We move on. We keep going. We are greater than the car, and we were never defined by the car. We are defined by what we take with us once we leave the car behind. We outlast the car.

Everything in my experience tells me that we outlast our bodies. We move on. We keep going. We are bigger than our bodies. What defines us is what we take with us once we leave our bodies behind—our joys, our dreams, our loves, our consciousness.

We are not bodies with souls.

We are souls with bodies.

Our souls endure. Our consciousness endures. The energy that powers us endures. The Other Side, then, is the place our souls go when our bodies give out.

That raises a lot of questions. Is the Other Side a place? Is it a sphere? A realm? Is it material or spiritual? Is it a way station or a final destination? What does it look like? How does it feel? Is it full of golden clouds and pearly gates? Are there angels? Is God there? Is the Other Side heaven?

I came by my understanding of the Other Side slowly, and even today I'm sure I know only a small part of what there is to know about it. But we don't need to fully envision or understand the Other Side in order to take great comfort from it. In fact, so many of us already believe our loved ones who've passed are still with us—in spirit, in our hearts, called back into our lives through memories. And that belief is endlessly nourishing.

The reality of what happens when our loved ones pass on, however, is infinitely more comforting than most people realize, because these departed souls are much closer than we think.

Here are the first two truths I learned through my gift:

1. Our souls endure and return to a place we call the Other Side, and
2. The Other Side is really very close.

How close? Try this—take an ordinary sheet of paper in your hand. Now hold it up in front of you, as if you're reading from it. Notice how that sheet of paper becomes a border that neatly divides the space it inhabits. It may be sheer and flimsy, a few tiny pulp fibers strung together, but it's still inarguably a border. In fact, as a border, it divides a great amount of molecules, atoms, and subatomic particles. When you hold it up in front of you, you and billions of things are on one side, and billions of other things—chairs and windows and cars and people and parks and mountains and oceans—are on the other.

And yet, from your side of the paper, you can see and hear and access the other side quite easily—in fact, some of your fingers are already there, holding the paper. The sides may be separate, but, practically speaking, they are one and the same. The other side of the paper is *right there*.

As you come across the term "Other Side" in this book keep that sheet of paper in mind. Ask yourself, *What if the border between our earthly life and an afterlife is as thin and permeable as a single piece of paper?*

What if the Other Side is right there?

2

The Girl in the Grocery Store

LONG BEFORE THE SWIMMING POOL incident, I was a strange little kid.

I was hyperactive and volatile. I had extreme reactions to ordinary things. "When Laura is happy, she is happier than any child I've ever seen," my mother wrote in my baby book when I was one year old. "But when she's sad, she is sadder than any child could ever be."

Plenty of children are fidgety and energetic, but I had a motor inside me that was constantly churning, and I had no way to shut it off. My first week of first grade, my mother got a call from the school nurse.

"I'll give you the good news first," the nurse said. "We were able to stop the bleeding."

I'd run into a ladder on the playground, cutting a bloody gash in my forehead. My mother took me to the doctor, who gave me seven stitches.

A week later I threw a nasty tantrum in my bedroom because my sister had been invited to a neighbor's pool and I wasn't. I knocked over the heavy, wooden bunk-bed ladder and it hit me on the back of the head. My mother took me back to the doctor, who gave me three more stitches and sat my mother down and asked her a lot of tough questions.

I was a tiny thing, undersized and stick-thin, a little blond moppet with bangs, but I could be a terror. My mother had to pin me down by an arm or a leg to get me dressed. If she let go of me for a second, I'd be gone. I constantly walked into things—doors, walls, mailboxes, parked cars. My mother would take her eyes off of me for a moment and the next thing she'd hear was a crash or a bonk. At first she'd hug me and comfort me, but after a while it became, "Oh, Laura Lynne walked into a wall again."

I'd get upset at my older sister, Christine, and I'd stomp my feet and put my head down and charge at her like a bull. Either I'd crash into her and knock her over, or she'd jump out of the way and I'd go flying.

"Go to your room," my mother would say to me, "and don't come out until you can be human again."

The worst punishment of all, though, was being told to sit still.

After I'd been particularly bad my mother would make me sit in a chair and not move. Not for an hour, or even ten minutes—my mother knew better than that. My punishment was to sit still for one minute.

And even that was way too long. I never made it.

We think of ourselves as solid, stable, physical beings. But we're not.

Like everything else in the universe, we are composed of atoms and molecules that are constantly vibrating with energy—constantly moving. These atoms and molecules vibrate at different intensities. When we look at a sturdy chair it doesn't seem like the atoms and molecules that compose it are moving at all. But they are. All matter, all creation, all life is defined by this vibrational movement. We are not as solid as we think we are. Essentially, we are energy. I guess my vibrational movements were a little more intense than other kids'.

Other than that, though, I had a pretty normal childhood. I grew up in a lovely, leafy, middle-class village called Greenlawn on Long Island. My father was a first-generation Hungarian immigrant who taught high school French, and my mother, whose parents came from Germany, was a high school English teacher who stayed home to raise her three children before going back to work.

We weren't poor, but money was tight. I had to wait to get haircuts and I wore my older sister's hand-me-downs. My mother dedicated herself to giving us kids the most wonderful childhood. If she couldn't afford new toys, she made amazing cars and trains and villages out of brightly painted cardboard. She drew little scenes and characters on our brown paper lunch bags every day. On holidays and birthdays she would decorate the entire house, and for one of Christine's parties she made pretty bonnets for her and all her friends. She kept us away from the TV and encouraged us to be creative. Christine and I would draw and paint, and we opened our own little art gallery (ten cents per masterpiece). My mother made my childhood feel magical.

Even so, there was no denying that I was difficult and different.

One day, when I was six, my mother took me with her to the grocery store. As we waited on the checkout line, I suddenly was overcome by emotion. I wanted to burst out crying. It was as if I was standing on a beach and a great big wave of emotion smashed into me and knocked me over—that's how powerful and unsettling it was. I stood there feeling unbearably sad and confused. I didn't say anything to my mother. Then my attention was drawn to the cashier.

She was young, maybe in her early twenties, and unremarkable. She wasn't frowning or crying. She looked bored. But I knew she wasn't just bored. I knew she was the source of this horrible sadness I was feeling.

It was unmistakable to me that I was absorbing the cashier's sadness. I didn't know what that meant or why it was happening. I didn't even know if it was unusual or not. All I knew was that I felt her sadness, that it was extremely uncomfortable and confusing, and that I had no way of shutting it off.

I would have many more experiences like that. Sometimes I'd walk by a stranger on the street and be hit by a powerful charge of anger or anxiety. Other times I'd absorb the emotions of my friends and classmates. Most of the time these experiences were difficult and unhappy. But I could feel happy emotions, too.

Whenever I was around someone who was especially happy, I felt positively elated. It was as if the emotions not only transferred to me but also intensified on the way over. Sometimes I'd experience sheer, unbridled joy in moments that clearly called for a less ecstatic response. Simple, happy moments—sharing ice cream with friends, swimming on a summer's day, sitting with my smiling mother—could flood me with euphoria and make my spirits soar.

Today I can still summon those moments of bliss, and my tendency to hyperrespond is still there. Sometimes just hearing a song or reading a poem or seeing a painting, or even taking a bite of something delicious makes me feel an explosion of joy and well-being. It's as if, in those simple moments, I most acutely feel my connection to the world.

When I was a child it meant that I'd go from extreme happiness to dire depression, depending on whom I was near. I'd have deep plummets, followed by sky-high exuberance, followed by yet another dive—a roller coaster of mood swings. I came to expect these wild emotional shifts and learned to wait them out until I could regain my balance.

The realization that I was absorbing other people's feelings was a big step toward understanding why I was so emotionally volatile. But it would be years before I realized this strange ability of mine was actually not that strange and that it had a name—empathy.

Empathy describes our capacity to understand and share the emotions of others. There have been groundbreaking scientific experiments, particularly by two neuroscientists, Giacomo Rizzolatti and Marco Iacoboni, that demonstrated that the brains of some animals and nearly all humans contain cells called mirror neurons. Mirror neurons fire during both the execution and the perception of an activity. "If you see me choke up from emotional distress, mirror neurons in your brain simulate my distress," Iacoboni explained. "You know how I feel because you literally feel what I am feeling."

Empathy is one of the ways we are profoundly connected as human beings. It's the reason we experience joy when our favorite team wins—because, even though we aren't playing the game ourselves, we happily absorb the elation of the players. It's the reason we are moved to donate money to victims of tragedies a world away—because we can put ourselves in the shoes of a stranger and feel his or her distress.

In other words, human beings are meaningfully and crucially connected to each other. There are real and vital pathways between us.

At first I experienced these pathways as shared sadness and happiness. Later I would see cords of light binding us together. My understanding that we are all connected began that day in the grocery store, and every experience that followed deepened that understanding of the light between us.

3

Australia

BY THE TIME POP POP passed away, I was already aware I had a powerful connection to the people around me—so powerful that I couldn't escape their feelings and emotions. But after Pop Pop died and I saw him in that dream, I began to realize that I was also connected in some way to people who had crossed.

All of this was very confusing. Though seeing Pop Pop again was a gift, my abilities still felt more like a curse than a blessing. They confused me and often overwhelmed me. What did these connections mean, and why was I able to perceive them? Was I just weird and different? Or was something else at work? I needed to find a name for what was wrong with me. That's when, without really knowing what the word meant, I came up with a diagnosis. I went up to my mother one day when she was loading the dishwasher and said, "Mom, I think I'm psychic."

I don't remember when or how I learned what a psychic was. Maybe it was something I saw in a TV show or read about in a book. Certainly I didn't fully understand what it meant. But it was enough for me to know a psychic could see into the future. Wasn't that what I could do?

My mother stopped loading dishes and looked down at me. All of a sudden, I let it all out—I told her everything. About knowing that Pop Pop was going to die and how I saw him in a dream, and about all my guilt and fear. And as I spoke I felt myself start to cry.

"What is wrong with me?" I asked my mother. "Am I a bad person that I knew that? Was it my fault that he died? Am I cursed? Why can't I just be normal?"

My mother put her hand on my shoulder and sat me down at the kitchen table. Then she took my hands in hers.

"Listen to me," she said. "It's not your fault that Pop Pop died. You are not cursed. You have nothing to feel guilty about. You just have an extra ability—that's all."

It was the first time I heard my condition referred to as an ability.

"It's just a part of you, and every part of you is beautiful," my mother said. "It's a natural thing. Don't be afraid of it. The universe is bigger than we think."

Then my mother told me something that changed everything. The abilities I had, it seemed, ran in her family for generations.

Her mother, Babette, whom I knew as Omi, was one of ten children raised in a tiny village nestled in the mountains of Bavaria. When Omi was young, powerful thunderstorms got trapped between the mountains and unleashed their fury over the valley. Often my grandmother's parents would wake her in the middle of the night and get her dressed so she would be ready to flee should lightning strike their house.

The seclusion of her village limited Omi's contact with the outside world. There were no telephones, no radios. Omi was raised on legends, folklore, and superstitions. She was taught that seeing a spider before breakfast meant a long day of bad luck. Passing a sheep on the left was good luck, but passing on the right, not so much. She knew to never put her shoes on the table lest she invite bad tidings, and if she unnecessarily turned on lights during the day she made the angels cry. If she forgot something at home, she had better turn around three times, sit down, and count to ten before resuming her journey once she retrieved it.

Worst of all was finding a bird inside a house. That meant certain death for someone close.

Early on, Omi also learned to trust in the power of dreams. She found that sometimes a similar presence would appear in her dreams—a dark figure who would press his face to the window and hold up three fingers. She hated those dreams. After having them, Omi would announce the next morning that something bad was going to happen in three days. Almost always she was right: a setback, an accident, a death.

"I was waiting for that," she would say. "At least now it's over."

Omi eventually moved to America, married, and raised a family that included my mother, Linda, and my aunt Marianna. But her dreams followed her across the ocean. One night she was awakened by a frightening dream in which a close friend in Germany died. She wrote down the date and time. A short while later Omi received a letter postmarked from Germany alerting her of the death of this person, who had died on the same day and at the same hour that Omi had recorded.

Another morning, Omi was sitting in her kitchen braiding nine-year-old Marianna's hair. My mother was seven years old. Suddenly the telephone rang.

Before Omi could answer it, Marianna blurted out, "They're calling from Germany to tell you Uncle Karl died."

"Shush!" Omi scolded her. "That's a horrible thing to say."

She picked up the phone and listened for a minute, and then her face went white. The call was from Germany. Omi's brother Karl had died.

My mother wondered how Marianna could have possibly known this. She and her sister didn't even know they had an uncle Karl. But this prediction was never discussed further. Throughout my mother's childhood, Omi had a special deck of cards that she kept hidden away. German and very old, they were akin to tarot cards. Every now and then, usually on Sunday afternoons, if one of her cousins came to visit and asked her to take out the cards, Omi would lay them on the table and interpret them in search of that person's fortune, good or bad.

Yet every time she took out the cards, she did so with a stern warning. The cards were not to be treated lightly, because every time you used them your guardian angels would abandon you for the next three days.

My grandmother believed that otherworldly energies and dream communications were real. Almost without exception, the messages that came through told of deaths or sickness or trouble. Because they were warnings of bad things that were about to happen, they were not welcomed or celebrated, just accepted.

Years later, when I announced to my mother that I was psychic, she told me about her own dreams. One time when she was in college, she had just gotten into bed and was falling asleep when she heard—clearly heard—her father call out her mother's name, but the way he said it somehow communicated alarm. Clearly there was something wrong! My mother sat up in bed, shaken and confused. Nothing like this had ever happened to her before. It was too late to call home that night, but early the next morning she phoned to ask "Is Daddy okay?" Her father had been finishing their basement, putting up knotty-pine paneling. He used a powerful table saw to cut the pieces needed, and the night before, as he guided a plank through the spinning blade, something slipped and his finger was cut deeply. And at that exact moment, he had yelled out for my grandmother to come. He was okay, but it was a dreadful cut.

When she was a bit older, she dreamed a neighbor had taken a terrible fall in a grocery store. When she awoke she had the urge to call the neighbor to see if he was okay, but she didn't. Later that day, she learned the neighbor had fallen and died.

———

There was also a dream about a red telephone. "In my dream this red telephone was ringing loudly and urgently, and I was trying desperately to answer it but I couldn't," my mother said. "The next day I found out your father's uncle had died in Hungary. Hungary was a communist country, and communism is associated with red. That's why the phone in my dream was red." She explained that there was often symbolism in psychic dreams or visions.

Aunt Marianna had her own stories that she shared with me after my confession. She told me how she would often get flashes of vision right before Christmas, and she would know exactly what her present would be. One time she had a vision of a small throw rug in the shape of a sunflower, and three days later, that's exactly what she found under the tree.

Marianna also had intense feelings of foreboding, where she'd know something bad was about to happen. Sure enough, a few days later, the bad thing would happen, and she'd say, just like Omi, "Oh God, I'm glad that's over."

But Marianna also had good, positive visions. Not long after Omi passed, Marianna saw a ladybug and recognized it as a message from her mother. Over the years, when she needed to feel her mother's love, a ladybug would magically appear. My mother sees them as well, and she, too, believes they are signs from her mother. She saw a ladybug fly into the room just before my aunt was headed to the hospital to have surgery. This past Christmas, she found a ladybug crawling across her kitchen floor—which was remarkable because you just don't see many ladybugs in the middle of winter in New York. Both my aunt and mother came to accept that our loved ones who have crossed are around us on earth all the time, still reaching out to us.

My aunt's long career as a nurse reinforced her belief that our loved ones on the Other Side are watching over us and bringing us comfort. Often her sickly patients would report, "My mother is sitting with me now." Or she'd hear them start talking to people in the room that no one else could see, people who had passed on years before. Marianna always knew what that meant: that the patient would be crossing soon. She found nothing odd about these sightings. Instead, she found them comforting—a validation that our loved ones often come to help us cross over to the Other Side. So when her patients said a relative was there, my aunt would just say, "Well, tell them hello and welcome them in."

Every time my aunt or mother shared one of these stories with me, I soaked it up with something like joy. They were not the least bit skeptical about these dreams and visions and messages. That is why my mother was so accepting of my premonition about Pop Pop.

Years later, when I was a teenager, my mother and aunt gave me a present. It came in an old gray felt jeweler's pouch. I reached inside and pulled out some cards—Omi's special cards.

They were colorful and vibrant, and the drawings on the cards were magical. There were swords and shields and kings and elephants. A cherub holding a beer stein. A boar carrying a dog. I was fascinated by how unique and vivid these images were. When my aunt sat me down and explained the symbolic meaning of each card, I recognized that what I was holding in my hands was a brand-new language. A way to find meaning that hadn't been there before.

I didn't use the cards all that much back then, and I still don't, because I seem to have my own connections with the Other Side. But the cards can be valid tools for some people. They can quiet the brain and help us focus on a new language of perception in order to receive information. I believe that's how Omi used them.

By giving the cards to me, my mother and aunt were essentially encouraging me to explore what's out there, to swim in it, and search for meaning. And in this way they let me know that I wasn't a freak, that there was nothing wrong with me, that what I had was something rooted deeply in the history of my family.

"Every part of you is legitimate," my mother once told me. "Every part of you deserves to be explored. Don't be afraid of your ability. It is real and it's a part of who you are."

On the day I finished sixth grade, nine months after Pop Pop died, my mother handed me another small present.

"This is from Pop Pop," she said.

I froze. What did she mean, the gift was from Pop Pop? I knew that when he was alive he took great pride in buying us beautiful gifts to mark special occasions. He was always celebrating life in some way. But how could this gift be from him?

My mother saw the look on my face and explained that my grandfather had bought it for me before he passed. He'd planned to give it to me when I graduated from elementary school.

I held the present in my hands. It was a small, delicate box, wrapped in plain brown paper with a burlap string around it—the way Pop Pop lovingly wrapped everything. I sat down and opened it carefully.

And when I saw what it was, I was astonished.

It was a beautiful silver bracelet with several panels on it. On each panel was the name of a city in Australia.

I slipped the bracelet on my wrist and touched the names of the cities with my fingers. Was it just a coincidence that both the bracelet and my dream about Pop Pop had to do with Australia? Or was there some deeper meaning to it? After all, neither of us had ever been there. It seemed totally random. And yet there it was, connecting us even after his death.

Was this Pop Pop's way of telling me, *I'm still with you, kid*?

All these years later, I still have vivid dreams about Pop Pop. These dreams feel especially real, like they're actually happening. I call them 3-D dreams. And in these dreams, I feel light as air, as if I'm no longer in my body. And always there is Pop Pop, as radiant with joy and light as ever. We visit and talk and just hang out, and though I don't remember what we talk about, I remember distinctly that being with him is beautiful.

And always, when I wake from these dreams, I am crying. A little out of sadness, because I still miss him. But mostly out of joy and love and happiness, because I know Pop Pop and I are still *connected*.

4

The Crush

WHEN I WAS TWELVE my mother's friend Arlene dropped by for a visit. I ran to the front door to greet her. I liked Arlene; she was fun and cheerful and always happy to see me. But on this day, when she walked in, I was taken aback.

The instant I saw her I heard a very distinct sound—a gentle, pleasant tinkling, like a glass chime dancing in the wind. Except there was no chime and there was no wind. Then, the instant I heard Arlene say hello, I saw a beautiful, swirly mix of bright colors around her.

I had no idea what I was hearing or seeing.

When my mother and Arlene sat down, I told them what had happened.

"Oh," Arlene said with a smile, "you're very psychic, aren't you?"

And that was that. The two of them went back to talking and laughing. I don't know if they didn't quite believe me or if they just didn't think it was a big deal. But to me, it was a very big deal. Because now I wasn't just feeling other people's energy; I was also hearing and seeing it.

From then on I had the ability to see people in colors. It didn't always happen, but it happened often enough that I got used to it. There is a technical name for this phenomenon—synesthesia. According to *Scientific American*, synesthesia is "an anomalous blending of the senses in which the stimulation of one modality simultaneously produces sensation in a different modality." For example, some synesthetes hear colors; others feel sounds or taste shapes.

By some estimates it's a rare phenomenon, present in only one out of every twenty thousand people. But some scientists believe it's much less rare, and may actually be possible for one out of every two hundred people. A synesthete may hear a note of music and taste broccoli, or read a line of black-and-white numbers and see them all in different colors. I didn't know anything about synesthesia back when I was twelve. All I knew was that I had yet another weird ability.

Somehow my brain was superimposing the colors onto physical reality. It was as if I were looking at an object through a tinted window—the color was in the glass, not on the object. Nor would the colors linger; they'd come to me in a flash and disappear just as suddenly. The ability was harmless and sometimes even amusing. "That person is blue," I'd say to myself with a giggle. Or "Does that woman know she's purple?"

Eventually I discovered I was more likely to be drawn to someone who was blue, say, than someone who was red. The blue colors gave me a sense of peace and happiness, while red felt angry and negative. And in this way I began to realize the colors were offering me a quick, convenient way to read people—to size up their energy and decide if I wanted to be around them. It was like having an extra sense to help me navigate the world. After all, I would decide what sweater to wear based on its color. That's something all of us do, all the time. Certain colors make us feel good, others don't.

The only difference for me was that, in addition to sweaters, people came in colors, too.

Around this time I got my first crush on a boy. His name was Brian and he was in my sixth-grade class. Whenever I was near him, I found that I really, really liked his energy. It was a new and completely exhilarating feeling. My crush stayed secret for a while, until I told my friends about it, and then they told Brian's friends, and after that I assumed he knew I liked him. But then, through the same grapevine, word came back that Brian didn't like me—he liked my friend Lisa. I was crushed.

I was also extremely confused. It didn't make sense that I could be so drawn to him without him feeling the same pull. "But I really like his energy," I'd tell myself. "How can that not *mean* something?" The let-down and frustration were so painful. I know all unrequited crushes are devastating for girls and boys that age, but what I felt was beyond just liking someone—I felt connected to Brian.

Eventually I got over Brian and, in the seventh grade, developed an equally powerful crush on a classmate named Roy. Once again, word came back that Roy liked my friend Leslie, not me. This time the confusion and disappointment were unbearable. I just couldn't understand why this pull I felt wasn't leading to anything. How could I feel so connected to Roy if I wasn't meant to be with him? Night after night I sat in my bedroom in the dark and tried to shut off my feelings, but I couldn't. I just wanted to disappear so I didn't have to feel so intensely anymore.

As I got older, the intensity of these feelings began to work both ways. If a boy liked me but I didn't like him back, I'd feel utterly miserable. It's an uncomfortable situation for anyone, but for me it was more than just knowing a boy liked me—I would feel his energy, and absorb all his sadness. I didn't have the luxury of shrugging anything off—these typical teenage interactions were all-consuming and sometimes even crippling for me.

And so, as I entered my teenage years and developed relationships beyond my family members, my abilities became even more confusing. They weren't always negative, though. On my first day in eighth grade, in art class, I suddenly felt my attention pulled clear across the room to a girl with brown hair and green eyes. It felt like someone or something was tugging on me. The girl's name was Gwen, and she wasn't someone I'd have felt inclined to approach. She was deep in conversation with her friend Margie, and she had a scowl on her face. Still, I felt a click, as if our energies were locking together, so I got up and walked over and said hello. She gave me a puzzled look, as if to say, *Who are you and why are you talking to me?* But I didn't budge.

And before long, Gwen and I were best friends.

Our friendship lasted all through high school and beyond. To this day, she is my oldest friend and we are still part of each other's lives. We cheer each other on and comfort each other when things aren't great. We like to say we're just each other's "cup of tea."

When I was fifteen my family went on a ski trip to Mt. Sutton in Quebec, about a nine-hour drive from our home. We were with some family friends: Mr. Smith, an English teacher who worked with my father (we called him Uncle Lee), his wife, Nancy, and their sons, Damon and Derek, plus Damon's friend Kevin. Kevin was two years older than me, six feet tall with blond hair and a thin build. Instantly I loved his energy. It was happy, unassuming, warm, gentle, and safe. I felt like I knew him, even though we'd just met.

We were staying at a condo near the ski resort, and one evening we all went to a little bistro next door. Kevin and I sat next to each other and started talking. And as we did, the space around us suddenly went silent, and I felt an incredible merging of energy. It felt like something had just been decided. The energy of the space between us shifted and linked, and I felt something like a magnetic pull. It was astonishing. I'd never felt anything like it before.

Then it was time to leave. I felt my own energy swirling madly around inside of me, but I tried to find my balance and play it cool. In the doorway, just as we were about to step outside into the cold, Kevin turned, smiled softly, leaned down, and kissed me. On the lips.

It was my first kiss. And my world exploded.

The kiss gave me permission to dive headfirst into Kevin's energy field. It was an invitation for me to swoop right in. That had never happened before, either—other people's emotions were always something I had to wrestle with or fight off. But not with Kevin. With Kevin, I welcomed it. The feeling was exhilarating. I fell madly in love.

We spent many happy months together as girlfriend and boyfriend. Yet despite our intense connection, my easy access to Kevin's inner self revealed something unexpected—Kevin and I weren't meant to stay together. From very early on I could sense that his path in life was inevitably going to stray from mine. I was falling in love with books and reading, while Kevin liked tinkering with cars and electronics. I still loved him, and I could tell he was a beautiful, caring soul, but I knew we were meant to go our separate ways.

Maybe that's something a lot of people can sense even when

they're in loving relationships. But I did more than sense it—I knew it with something like absolute certainty.

My breakup with Kevin wasn't especially dramatic, and to this day I still love him for the person he is. He was my first love, and that alone makes him very special to me.

But my teenage romance was also an important life lesson: loving someone and feeling that he or she is your soul mate does not necessarily mean you are meant to be together forever.

We can love someone's soul and at the same time understand that we are not meant to stay with that person. Sometimes the end of a relationship isn't a failure at all, but rather a release for both people so that they can travel on their own true paths. Some relationships are only meant to teach us lessons about love.

I also learned that we can let people go on their paths while still wishing them love. There doesn't need to be bitterness, blame, and anger. Over the years I've run into Kevin a few times, and it brings my heart great joy to know he is happily married with three beautiful kids. Kevin has a life that he loves, and that was everything I wished for him to find.

Not long after I broke up with Kevin, I fell in love again. His name was Johnny, and he was in my tenth-grade class at John Glenn High School on Long Island. Johnny was the badass of the class. He was six feet tall, with pale skin, brown hair, and blue eyes. He was a jokester, always laughing and pulling pranks, but he was also tough and got into lots of fights. He seemed more confident, alive, and adventurous than most boys his age. And because of that, everyone was drawn to him.

The first time we spoke was on Halloween night, when I was with a group of friends at a local hangout we called the "El Streets"—the corner of Elmundo and Elkhart. I wasn't wearing a costume; I probably thought I was too cool for it. Johnny was wearing a black leather jacket. We caught each other's eye and he came over and we talked, and as we did I felt his powerful, positive energy wash over me. Before I knew it, I was completely lost in it. Johnny didn't even have to kiss me to throw open the doors. All he had to do was stand near me.

Diving into his energy field, I found that Johnny's emotions were laid bare for me in a way I'd never experienced before—I could read him, as the saying goes, like an open book. I could tell that beneath his hypermasculine façade Johnny was nursing some very deep wounds. I learned that his parents had divorced when he was young, and Johnny grew up with very little attention from either parent. He was pretty badly neglected by all the adults in his life, and he desperately needed to feel loved.

I saw through his tough-guy act right away. When Johnny realized how attuned I was to who he was deep down, he poured everything out to me—his background, his fears, his dreams. Not surprisingly, we fell in love.

My relationship with Johnny revealed yet another troubling facet of my abilities. Because I could so clearly feel his pain and hurt, I also felt a powerful urge to fix those things.

When I told my mother, who was an English teacher at my school, that I was dating Johnny, she said, "That boy? Don't you dare date him. He gave me the finger once when I was on bus duty."

But when I brought Johnny home and my mother talked with him, she quickly came to love him, too. She saw, as I did, the wounded little deer inside him—the part that was lonely and hurt—and wanted to help him any way she could. Over the next few years, Johnny became like a member of our family.

Our relationship lasted a couple of years, but like a lot of high school couplings, it was bumpy. What drew me to him—his buried pain and torment—was also what made things volatile. We broke up, got back together, then broke up again. That was the nature of our relationship. Even our soul-deep connection was not enough to save us.

Eventually I realized that I was so plugged into Johnny's intense emotional landscape that our relationship would always be intolerably complicated. I knew we had no real chance of ever truly meshing and understood that our time together was up.

I still think of Johnny with love. Our time together furthered my awareness that people are brought into our path for a reason. There is always something to be taught or to be learned, either for one of you or for both. And I am happy to say that his path led him to be a happily married father of two children. It brings my heart great joy to know that.

My abilities didn't necessarily make my dating years easier to navigate, but they did help me begin to understand the bigger picture. Slowly I was starting to piece together a kind of inventory of my abilities. I didn't have names for them and I didn't fully understand what they meant or how to use them. But every time I discovered a new one, my self-awareness grew.

Somehow I could read people's energies and absorb their emotions. I could see colors around people and use those colors to help me understand the world around me. I had the ability to look into people's lives and know things about them, like how many siblings they had or if their parents were divorced. I had dreams that were impossibly vivid, and these dreams were full of messages that meant something to me in the real world.

All these abilities have names I now know, but back then I only knew them as the things that gave my life a confusing and often overwhelming intensity. I didn't even know if they were unique to me or if everyone had them.

What was undeniable was that as I grew into my teens, the energy inside me grew more intense. I looked for ways to power down my relentless internal motor, but nothing seemed to work. This energy, I suspect, would have consumed every facet of my life had I not found an unlikely outlet for it: soccer.

When I was in fourth grade I started playing soccer. Very quickly it became my salvation. I was plopped down in the middle of a great big field and told to run to my heart's content. Playing soccer gave me a sense of freedom and openness, and in the process, it allowed me to expend some of my crazy energy.

I got pretty good at it. I played in a travel soccer league, and in junior high I made the varsity team. Even though I was undersized, I held my own. Soccer meant more to me than it did to other kids. It wasn't just a hobby for me; I had no choice but to be relentless out there. But I had another advantage on the field—my abilities.

I found that I could read the energy of players on the opposing team. I'd line up on the left or right wing and take a look at the defender nearest me, and in an instant I'd know something about her that helped me decide my next move. *That girl is really aggressive,* I'd think. *Let me charge her and fake her out, and she'll bite on the fake and I'll get by her.* Or I'd see a defender I sensed was more passive and think, *Go right at her and she won't be able to keep up.* Sometimes the entire left half of the soccer field felt open and inviting to me, so I'd dribble the ball down the left side and reach the goalie easily. I scored a ton of goals.

Was I cheating? Sometimes it felt that way. But in the end, there was nothing I could do about it. I knew what I knew, and that's just the way it was. I couldn't shut off my abilities, so why not use them for something constructive? I got so good that I was often written up in the local paper.

"Laura bolted up and down the field today," the article would read. "Her energy is unstoppable."

If they only knew.

5

John Moncello

THANKS TO SOCCER I made it through school. I still didn't know how to control my abilities, but along the way I learned how to hide them. No one knew about the flood of emotions and the strange colors and the intense dreams, and I worked hard to keep it that way.

I enrolled at Binghamton University, a top-notch state school about two hundred miles northwest of New York City. College would be the first time I'd ever lived away from home, and that was both scary and exciting. I was sad to leave my parents, but I also felt like leaving home was a chance to establish an identity free of all the weirdness of my childhood.

What I didn't anticipate was how college life would affect me. There were so many students packed into such a small space, I felt like I was caught in a tornado of new ideas and new emotions and new energy. Between my dorm room and the communal bathroom I'd pass five new people, each of them buzzing and bristling with new energy. I'd nod or say hello, but at the same time I'd feel blasted by whatever it was they were feeling at that moment. A moment later I'd feel blasted again by the next student I passed. Fear, anxiety, sadness, excitement, loneliness—it was a barrage of emotion unlike anything I'd ever experienced before. I felt like a giant human tuning fork, vibrating with the collective energy of hundreds and hundreds of emotionally turbulent young people.

I was also being exposed to extraordinary works of art and history and political thought—a beautiful piece of music, a classic painting, a dynamic lecture, a mind-bending poem. All of that raised my spirits to unprecedented heights. Quite often I felt such soaring, unbridled joy over something, I'd have to remind myself to breathe. But then just walking out of a classroom and past a student who was depressed could knock me right off my high and plunge me into an abyss. It was like wading in a stream with constantly shifting currents and temperatures—one moment the water was choppy and frigid, the next it was peaceful but boiling hot. I couldn't understand what was happening, and I certainly couldn't stop it. All I could do was stay in the water and try to keep from drowning.

During winter break, I went back home to Long Island and reconnected with some of my high school friends. A bunch of us rented a room in the hotel where we'd held our senior prom, and we sat around and drank and talked about our college experiences. I gravitated toward a really good friend named John Moncello.

John was one of the most beautiful and dynamic human beings I ever met. We'd known each other since the day he'd stuck a note in my backpack in the fourth grade telling me he liked me and asking me to go roller-skating. We never dated—for whatever reason I turned down his artful proposal—but I always considered us great friends, and I always felt pulled to and linked to his energy. That energy was just so wonderfully, wildly positive. He was one of the smartest kids in school, and he was one of those people who made you feel comfortable in your own skin. All of us thought of John as the leader of our little group.

That night during winter break, John and I sat in a corner of the hotel room and swapped stories about Binghamton and Berkeley, where he was a freshman. As the night wore on, and everyone else passed out or went to sleep, John and I stayed up late, talking. It had always been that way with us. We'd find ourselves absorbed in incredible, deep conversations—the kind of talks I never had with my other friends. That night, John and I talked about the nature of existence. Suddenly John got quiet and looked out at the dark sky.

"What do you think happens when we die?" he asked.

"Well," I said, "I know there is a heaven."

"How do you know?"

"I just know," I said. "I know there is an afterlife. And I know that's where we go when we die."

John looked at me and furrowed his brow. I felt the urge to tell him about my Australia dream, and seeing Pop Pop, and all the other strange things that had happened to me, but I held back. John smiled and laughed.

"Laura, maybe I'll believe that when I'm older," he said, "but I'm young, so I don't have to worry about that yet. For now, I just don't believe in an afterlife."

I didn't say anything to try to convince him otherwise. I wasn't in any position to. We left it at that. A few days later we went back to school.

About a month after returning to campus, I had another intense and impossibly vivid dream.

In the dream I was in college—not Binghamton but somewhere else. And in the dream I became someone else, and I felt myself about to lose consciousness. I tried to call out for help, but no words came out. I had the horrible sense that if I couldn't get help, I would die. But no matter what I tried to do, I couldn't stop slipping away.

Then, all of a sudden, I was me again. I saw a group of my friends from high school walking somberly outside my dorm room. They were crying and carrying something on their shoulders. Some kind of box. The box was closed, and I couldn't see what was in it, but I didn't have to see. I knew right away there was a person in the box. A boy. A boy we loved. Our leader.

As I stood there and watched the procession reach me, I felt sheer, absolute terror, because I knew that if I didn't do something—or rather, undo something—my friends would suffer greatly, because this boy we loved so very much would be gone.

Then I woke up.

I sat up, breathing hard and in a panic, and looked at the digital clock on the nightstand. It read 12:00 noon on the nose. I grabbed my phone and frantically dialed my mother.

"Mom, did someone die?" I asked, half hysterically.

"What? No. What are you talking about?"

I recounted the dream, rushing through it and feeling the same kind of guilt and sorrow I'd felt after finding out my grandfather had died.

"Laura, slow down, it's okay," my mother said.

"No, Mom, it's not okay!" I yelled, starting to cry. "Someone died or is going to die! Please don't leave the house! Don't go anywhere!"

I was panicked. I knew enough about these vivid dreams to know they were real. My mother talked me through it and calmed me down. She assured me that everyone in our family was okay. I spent the rest of that day praying my phone wouldn't ring. And as the hours passed without bad news, my anxiety lessened just a bit.

At eight o'clock that night my phone rang. It was one of my high school friends.

"Laura, I have something horrible to tell you," he said. "John Moncello is dead."

=====

John had been pledging a fraternity at Berkeley and he'd been drinking the night before, quite a bit. In the middle of the night, around 3:00 a.m., some frat brothers called him and told him to come over to the frat house right away. "You have to clean up the place, pledge," they told him. John protested, saying he was too drunk to go. The brothers insisted, so John put on some clothes and staggered to the house.

He did his best to clean up the place, and when he was done he climbed out a window onto the fire escape. The frat boys often left the house via the fire escape. But John was still drunk, and he slipped and stumbled. He fell three stories and landed in the driveway.

No one saw him fall. No one knew he was there. So he lay on the asphalt, unconscious and bleeding. Someone found him there a few hours later. By then he was dead.

The coroner's report said John bled to death due to head trauma. He had died not from the fall but rather from a loss of blood. His body was discovered at precisely 9:00 a.m. Pacific Time. That was 12:00 noon in New York—the moment I woke up from my dream.

The coroner also reported that John had likely drifted in and out of consciousness for a while. Either he was unable to call for help or he did but no one heard him.

But I had heard him.

=====

I was destroyed. I completely lost my composure on the phone with the friend who called with the news. I blurted out my dream to him. I felt so dark and cursed. This was the affirmation that whatever was wrong with me—whatever the source of my abilities—it had to be something evil. How could I be given this information about my friend John yet not have the ability to change the outcome? Why have the dream but not be able to act on the information to save someone's life? What kind of sick, horrific, impotent ability was this?

The day after learning of John's death I left Binghamton and drove back home to Long Island. I met up with some high school friends, and we went to John's house to pay our respects to his mother.

She was distraught and in shock. She piled up all of John's college things in the living room. She told us that if we wanted any of his things, we could just take them. I watched some of my friends descend on his stuff—T-shirts, books, CDs, sneakers. The sight of that made me feel ill. *Please stop!* I wanted to yell out. But I didn't say anything. I stood there and felt even more isolated.

The next day was a blur. During the funeral procession the hearse carrying John's body drove slowly past his home—past the place where his dreams and hopes had been shaped. The funeral mass felt surreal, as if I were watching a movie. The speeches about what an amazing person John was did nothing to lighten my grief; instead they magnified the finality of his passing. John was gone. He wasn't coming back. And among this devastated group of people who loved him there was, perhaps, only one person who had known his life was slipping away before it actually did. Why couldn't I have saved him?

The immense guilt I felt was the reason I finally decided to start talking about my dream. I guess I was hoping I would discover that someone else had "known." I told three or four friends, in separate conversations, about the dream, and they all listened politely, but it was clear it didn't mean anything to them. It was just a dream, after all, and what do dreams have to do with the realities of life and death?

After that I stopped talking about my dream altogether. I internalized everything I was feeling. Maybe that was the way it was supposed to be. Maybe that would be my penance for not saving John.

=

We all have to figure out who we are and how we fit into this world. There were moments in my teenage years when I began to think that maybe my abilities were inseparable from and central to my ultimate purpose in life. I couldn't escape them and I couldn't make them stop, and so I entertained the idea that my purpose might be finding a way to control them and use them in the service of something good.

But John's death, and my dream about it, changed all that.

There was no possible way my purpose in life could involve something so painful and so difficult and so wrenching as this. That kind of "knowing" couldn't be something good—it had to be something bad.

I vowed to turn my back on this so-called gift. I didn't want it. I didn't need it. I would live my life without it.

6

Litany Burns

AFTER JOHN'S FUNERAL and before I went back to Binghamton I made an appointment to see the pastor of my church on Long Island. I needed to talk to someone and my pastor was an obvious choice. He was a sweet, kind man, and I'd known him since I was a little girl. He was thin and had a beard, and he reminded me of Jesus. Maybe that's why I trusted him so much.

I met the pastor in his office in the back of the church, and as soon as I sat down I burst into tears. Through sobs and gasping for breath I told the pastor everything—about my dream and John's death. I told him about my grandfather and the weird impulse that made me go see him one last time. I scanned the pastor's face for any sign of judgment or dismissiveness, but there were none. He just sat and listened and let me tell my story. Finally, when I was done, he spoke.

"Laura, what classes are you taking in college?" he asked.

I told the pastor my schedule: literature, history, philosophy . . .

"You're taking a philosophy class?"

"Yes. Intro to Philosophy."

"Well, that's it," he said matter-of-factly. "The dreams, and how you interpret them, and all that—it's all related to your philosophy class. It's a factor of all the new ideas and theories that are filling your mind. The class made you have the dream."

I listened as he spoke, and I felt my tears dry up. I took a deep breath, thanked the pastor for his time, shook his hand, and left. He'd meant no harm, and surely in his heart he believed he was helping me. But it was instantly clear to me that what he was telling me wasn't right. After all, my abilities had been haunting me long before I ever signed up for Intro to Philosophy.

I would not find my answers in this church, or any church, I decided. I believed in God and I believed God held the answers, but after my talk with the pastor I also believed God was so much bigger and more powerful than this little brick-and-mortar church. The answers were out there, somewhere else.

Back at Binghamton I tried to slip into the rhythms of college life. I didn't tell anyone how distraught and unbalanced I felt—just as I didn't dare tell anyone about my abilities. I tried to be a typical freshman. I went to parties, studied hard, dated some boys. But I could not get the dream about John out of my mind, and I fell into a deep depression.

My friend Maureen was the one who came to my rescue.

Because she was my best friend in college, I'd told her a little bit about my abilities. One day she mentioned a woman she'd heard of who lived in the small river community of Nyack, just north of New York City, where Maureen was from.

"Her name is Litany Burns, and she is a psychic," Maureen said. "She worked on the Son of Sam case a few years ago. Maybe she can give you some answers."

I didn't waste a moment. I made an appointment with Litany Burns for a one-hour session. She was a clairvoyant, a channeler, and a healer, and back in 1977 she'd been invited by the Manhattan district attorney to work on the infamous Son of Sam case in New York City. She didn't advertise her services; apparently it was all word of mouth.

A week later, on a crisp March day, Maureen and I drove three hours to Nyack in her red convertible. Nyack is a small and pretty Hudson River town that seemed stuck in another century. Litany's office was in a modest two-story pale-brick building on a quaint corner on Main Street. We found a parking spot, and Maureen wished me luck and went shopping. I was anxious, excited, and a little scared. I walked up to the ground-floor entrance, but I hesitated before ringing the buzzer. My insides were churning. Finally I took a deep breath and rang the bell, and Litany let me in.

She greeted me at the door of her office. She was in her thirties, with shoulder-length blond hair and lovely, kind green eyes. She had a radiant energy that made me feel instantly at ease. I saw the color blue around her—a warm, healing blue. Being near her felt like standing next to a space heater on a freezing day. The nervousness drained right out of me.

We shook hands, and she led me to the sofa and sat in the chair opposite me. Her office was small and warm and plain. No hanging crystals or anything like that. Just a sofa and a chair and a desk. The walls were painted lavender. It was a safe, comforting place. At first Litany was quiet. She just looked at me and around me, as if she was sizing me up. Finally a slight smile appeared on her face.

"Well," she said in a soft, soothing voice, "I see you are one of us."

She was completely matter-of-fact, like a school nurse telling a child she has a fever. As for me, I sat there in disbelief.

"Do you know this?" Litany asked. "Do you know you are psychic?"

"No," I said. "I don't understand any of it. I just think I'm kind of a freak."

Litany smiled. "Do you feel things about people?" she asked. I nodded. "Do you read their energy?" Again I said yes. "Do you see and hear things that aren't seen or heard by others?" Yes to all of that.

"You are clairvoyant and clairaudient," Litany declared. "You have a gift, and in time you will understand how to use it. But the first step is not to be afraid of the gift. Do not feel cursed or ashamed. You are not a freak. Your gift is beautiful."

With those few words, Litany Burns began to make sense of my life. It was like having a heavy black curtain yanked away from a giant window, letting in a flood of glorious light. For the first time in my life I felt I'd met someone who understood me, not just superficially but from the inside out.

"You have a brother," Litany said. "And an older sister. Your father has a lot of emotion and he has a hard time showing it. Your mother is a strong force in your life."

Within minutes of meeting me she seemed to know everything about my family. Then she dug deeper.

"You are a sensitive, natural healer," she said, "and you are often drawn to someone who is not doing well. You want to make them better. I see you get a lot in dreams. You connect to the Other Side through your dreams."

As she spoke I felt enormous relief, but it was more than that—it was almost a sense of being forgiven. I had the sudden thought that maybe I'd heard John in my dream simply because I *could*. Not because I was cursed but because I was open to the Other Side and thus able to hear him. Maybe I had dreamed of John while he was dying not because I was meant to intervene or save him but because I was supposed to hear him say goodbye.

Litany continued, "You are mediumistic, too; what everyone else is feeling, you're feeling it, too. Even if they don't know they're feeling it."

I sat quietly, hanging on every word. Just a few minutes earlier I'd been hearing the sound of cars and trucks on Main Street, but now I couldn't hear anything except the sound of Litany's voice. It was like the rest of the world had shrunk away to nothing.

"You have always known, ever since you were a little child, that you were here to do something," she explained. "That you have a purpose. And this is the year of you beginning to understand that. That's why you are feeling such a push right now. You are here to help people. Don't be afraid of your power. All this is about you feeling comfortable enough with your loving and healing powers to truly feel them, and then act on them."

Toward the end of the reading Litany asked me if I had any questions. I reached into my purse and pulled out a photo of John. I wasn't sure why I'd brought the photo with me, but now I knew I had to show it to her.

"He's a boy," I said, my voice barely audible. "He was a friend. I brought this picture of him, and his death . . . he fell . . . they weren't sure what happened."

Litany held the photo for a minute before putting it down.

"It was an accident," she said. "He wasn't shoved or anything like that. Maybe there was drinking, but it was his own doing. There was no foul play."

Then Litany paused. Something about her changed, subtly but noticeably—her face, her eyes, her demeanor. She seemed to be somewhere else. I had no idea what was happening. Litany leaned forward.

"John is wanting you to say hi to his friends for him," she finally said. "He is saying, 'I am here. I'm okay. I just wish my mother could get over it. I keep coming around to see her and talk to her and help her, but she just doesn't hear me.'"

What was happening? Litany was speaking to me *as John*. In a way, she even sounded like him. Her mannerisms seemed like his, too. But how could that be?

"It's very neat here," she went on. "I can watch everyone and check them out. Physically, I miss people but I don't really feel like I'm away from everyone because I am here. I'm still here. I want you to know I am around. I know that you feel me. And I will keep coming around so you can feel me and know I'm here. And who knows, maybe one day I'll come back as somebody's kid."

Then Litany laughed. But it wasn't her laugh—it was John's laugh. And the crack about coming back as someone's kid was just the kind of thing John would say. Litany had never met John, yet she was bringing him to life right there in her small office in Nyack. I could feel his presence. I knew he was there.

"He is doing well," Litany said. "He has the same prankster personality he had here. He feels good—solid. He wants all of you to know he is doing okay, and that, most important, he still loves you all."

I lowered my head and began to cry.

More than anything else, I felt a soul-deep sense of relief.

It was relief that John was okay. But it was also relief that what I'd just witnessed—Litany somehow summoning John from wherever he was—was not at all something dark and twisted. It was good and forgiving and healing and loving! It was beautiful!

And in that moment, something clicked—something *changed*. I knew instantly this was a dividing line in my life.

Instead of feeling filled with fear, for the first time ever I felt filled with hope.

Before I left Litany gave me another gift, a book she'd written a few years earlier. It was called *Develop Your Psychic Abilities*. "It will explain a lot of things to you," she said. I felt like hugging her and not letting go, but instead I shook her hand and politely thanked her.

I ran down the stairs and found Maureen and told her what just happened. I was giddy, exhilarated. I felt free in a way I hadn't in years—maybe ever.

As soon as we got back to Binghamton I tore into Litany's book. With each page I felt wave after wave of recognition. "My God, this is me!" I'd yell to no one as I read it. "There are others! This has a name!"

I quickly finished Litany's book and went to the bookstore to find another one like it. I didn't know what I was looking for, but in the store I felt pulled to a particular book: *You Are Psychic: The Free Soul Method* by Pete A. Sanders Jr. It was written, oddly enough, by a biomedical chemistry and brain science scholar from the Massachusetts Institute of Technology. "By the time you finish reading this book," one early passage went, "the capacity to assess other people's temperaments and personalities, and the ability to sense, feel, hear, and see events before they happen can become everyday skills for you."

I kept reading—devouring—chapter after chapter, each one more enlightening than the last. There was even a chapter titled "Four Psychic Senses," the first of which was psychic intuition or, as the author called it, "knowing."

Knowing! Exactly what I called it! Knowing "is an inner awareness, unsupported by any particular internal sensation or external stimulus. You just know!"

My reading with Litany was a turning point in my life. Because of our meeting, instead of shutting down and trying to ignore my abilities, I began to embrace them. I worked on developing them and understood that they were a part of me—and that they were meant, somehow, to be a part of my path.

Litany made me feel less isolated, less freakish, and that alone was a miracle. Finally I was beginning to find answers. I was beginning to put the puzzle together. I was starting to see where and how I might fit in.

But I knew my reading with Litany wasn't meant simply to make me feel better about myself. The reading wasn't about my past. It was about my future.

"Use your talents," Litany told me as I was leaving. "Read people. Your gut will be a great friend to you, so follow it as much as you can. Follow it, use it, practice it.

"And when you do, you will be on your true path."

7

The Path Ahead

MY TIME WITH LITANY was not the end of my search for answers. In a way, it was just the beginning.

Everything she told me and everything I read in the books conveyed the same powerful message: be open. Open to new ideas, new streams of information, new possibilities. I may have understood my abilities a bit better, but I still didn't know how I was supposed to use them. So I kept digging.

In my junior year in college I came home for a visit and went to say hello to my mother's friend Arlene, whose colors I'd seen. I'd always been drawn to her open energy. Arlene was into astrology. I didn't know much about it, but when she suggested that she read my chart I was open to it.

The chart depicted the position of the planets, the moon, and the sun at the exact time of my birth. Arlene explained that by looking at these positions in the context of the twelve signs of the zodiac, she could gain insight into my life's path and purpose.

We sat at Arlene's kitchen table, and she made her judgments quickly and with authority. Many of Arlene's insights rang true—that I didn't like being told what to do, that I was both an introvert and an extrovert, and that I had a hard time containing all my energy.

Then Arlene said something that didn't make sense at all.

"Your sun is in semi-sextile and you're a Saturn," Arlene went on. "People trust you and respond to you. Tell me, are you thinking of being a teacher?"

A teacher? No, I didn't want to be a teacher. I had bigger plans. I was going to be a lawyer.

My older sister, Christine, was a brilliant undergrad at Princeton University who went on to earn a law degree from Harvard. She set the bar in our family. I figured I could be either a lawyer or a doctor, and since I hated math classes I had a better shot at being a lawyer.

I told Arlene about my plans, and she continued with the reading. But just a few minutes later she looked up and said, "I see a definite focus on teaching. It is part of your path. Somewhere down the line, teaching and education are going to be a part of what you do."

The chart is a little off, I thought, *because that's not going to happen.* I repeated to Arlene that I had just declared myself prelaw.

"Well," she finally said, "if that is true, then you will teach law, because teaching is what is set in your path."

The main thrust of the reading, though, was that I was destined to play a role in the world I couldn't yet see or understand.

"You are going to be serving humanity," Arlene said. "It will be something new, and something people will look for and find helpful. There is a gift you need to share with the world. It's just going to take some time for that to happen. It will not happen right away."

Arlene even knew how long it would take—sixteen years to

"pick up what you need from the universe," and another eight years after that to "make your move."

I loved hearing that I had some larger purpose in the world, but twenty-four years was just too far in the future for me to get too excited about it.

As the reading wound down, Arlene offered a suggestion.

"Let your mind roam," she urged. "Pick up all the things that are necessary for you to learn. Expect the unexpected. By doing that, you'll be setting down roots."

I felt a surge of excitement. Arlene's words were similar to what Litany had advised: *Use your talents. Read people. Follow your gut.* Now it was Arlene who was encouraging me to explore my abilities. She was validating that my search for answers wasn't misguided—that it was necessary for me to discover my true path.

I hugged Arlene. At the front door she smiled and said, "Happy adventure!"

Back at Binghamton, I developed a new way to deal with my abilities. While I no longer felt I had to hide them, I didn't want to parade them around, either. I didn't want to be the "psychic girl." I resolved I wouldn't let my psychic abilities define me; they would just be one part of who I was. They were just something I could do, like speaking French or playing soccer.

I loved the way being honest about my abilities made me feel. It was incredibly liberating. I was learning to integrate my gift into my otherwise normal life.

Treating my abilities so casually, however, had an unintended consequence. Without even realizing it, I wound up disrespecting them and using them in irresponsible ways.

One night I was having drinks with friends in a campus bar called The Rat. My abilities, I'd discovered, would open up after

I'd had two drinks of alcohol. It was like a magic formula. It even made sense to me, since alcohol shuts down the analytical mind, which for me made the psychic information that much more accessible. After a couple of drinks, information about people would just flood into me.

At The Rat, after my second drink, I looked across the bar and noticed a very cute boy. He was leaning against a wall, and he had brown curly hair peeking out from under his red baseball cap. He had a comfortable, masculine energy—confident but not arrogant. He was about five foot ten, with an athletic build, green eyes, and a casual, easy smile. I told my friend I was going to go over to talk to him.

"Good luck with Red Hat Boy," she said.

I sidled up to him and felt his aura pulling me in even closer.

"Hi," I said. "So your first name starts with a *J*?"

"Uh, yeah," he said. "Jeremy."

More information came through. "You have an older brother, right?" I said. "Two years older? And you have another brother who is, what, seven years old?"

Jeremy's easy smile started to fade.

"Oh, and you're Lutheran, right? Your whole family is Lutheran. Your dad isn't physically a presence in your life, but your mother is a forceful energy for you. You're very close with your mother. You always have been, and you're even closer now." I went on and on, telling Jeremy specific details about himself and his family. His jaw dropped about two inches.

"How . . . ?" he said. "Are you a stalker?"

"No," I said. "I'm just psychic."

I explained to Jeremy how I got information about people, and instead of being weirded out, he was open to it.

I used my abilities to pick up a guy.

I was trying to find a way that my abilities could be fun and useful and productive, not something that was dark and difficult.

I was seeing how my gift could come in handy, and even be a bit of a party trick. At times I didn't use it in the most honorable ways. There were a few occasions—not many, but a few—when, after I'd had a fight with someone, I might summon information about them, and if any of it was negative, I'd feel better knowing it. *She doesn't even realize her boyfriend is going to break up with her in three months,* I'd think, feeling smug. And if one of my good friends had a fight with someone, I'd "look" into that person and tell my friend, "Yeah, well, her parents are about to get divorced."

Looking back, I cringe at how inappropriately I used my abilities at times. Honestly, I wasn't trying to be cruel. I was only nineteen, and I was trying to figure out my life, just like any other girl that age. If I was reckless with my gift, it was because I didn't yet appreciate how special it was.

I was growing, learning, evolving. In high school I didn't really study hard or put much emphasis on academics. I did well grade-wise, but it wasn't because of hard work. At Binghamton, I took my studies much more seriously.

I had an English literature professor named David Bosnick, who became a mentor to me. His energy was enormous; the minute he walked into that classroom I was captivated. When I was around him I felt excited to be alive.

In my junior year he asked me to become his teaching assistant. I was honored and accepted right away.

Once a week I helped him devise assignments and grade papers, and I discovered I was pretty good at the business of class work. I taught my own discussion section of about twenty-five students, and I even graded the papers of students I knew—including seniors (who were a grade above me). At every step, Professor Bosnick subtly and not-so-subtly encouraged my interest in academia.

"The world has enough lawyers," he'd bellow. "Teach! Teach! *Teach!*"

I still had my sights on studying law, but decided I wanted to apply to study abroad for a semester at Oxford. "It'll be your senior year. Go somewhere else," my friends said. "Go party and have fun!" But Professor Bosnick had ignited a passion in me to keep learning—to be open to new ideas, to challenge myself academically. I didn't want to party. I wanted to study at Oxford.

8

Oxford

OXFORD WAS A TIME MACHINE back through the history of human energy and thought. It felt like this energy was everywhere around me. Here was where some of the boldest minds had searched for truth and wisdom. T. S. Eliot, the great scientist Linus Pauling, and dozens of other Nobel laureates had studied here. It was home to thousands of magical artifacts—ancient sundials and early telescopes, a Gothic astrolabe from the 1400s, a celestial globe from 1318, Mary Shelley's manuscript draft of *Frankenstein*, four original copies of the Magna Carta from 1215. Then there was the grand and revered Bodleian Library on Broad Street—one of the oldest libraries in existence. The "Bod," as it's been called for centuries, is magnificent. On my first trip there, I could hardly get past the entrance—a massive arched stone doorway carved with the coats of arms of several Oxford colleges. Once inside, I was staggered by the musty smell, the soaring arched ceilings, the gleaming mahogany desks, and endless wooden shelves packed tightly with ancient, leather-bound books.

And the books! Eleven million in all, every one imprinted with the power and energy of its creator. The writer Ezra Pound once said, "Man reading should be man intensely alive. The book should be a ball of light in one's hands." That is exactly how I felt when I first walked into the Bod—I felt the dazzling swirl of a million balls of light dancing around me, filling my spirit. I didn't feel like I was seeing the Bod for the first time. I felt like I was coming back to a place I belonged.

Quickly I settled into a comfortable routine. I was assigned to a little white flat at 66 Vicarage Road. My room looked out on a small garden, which had a magical fairy quality to it.

Every morning I'd get on a rusty blue bike I'd rented and ride to the Bod. I'd spend long hours writing, reading, and doing research into Shakespeare and Jane Austen, my two areas of study. At night I'd go to the local pub to meet friends for a late-night cider and black.

The academic program was rigorous, and it was the responsibility of the students to set their own course of study. I met with my two professors once a week. In those brief meetings we'd talk about my pace of study and my progress. The rest of the time I was on my own. I was expected to produce a paper at the end of every week. There was no coddling, no gentle encouragement. This was high-wire, sink-or-swim scholarship. I loved it. My time at Oxford was also powerfully legitimizing. No matter what weird abilities I had, Oxford confirmed that I also had the potential to accomplish great things academically. I worked harder than I ever had before, and I was challenged in a way I never had been. I spent nearly all my time immersed in learning and books. And I found that instead of sinking, I swam. Actually, I flew. In the end, my grades translated to an A+ in Shakespeare and an A in Jane Austen. Back in Bing-hamton I closed out my final college semester with a 4.0.

My days at Oxford were some of the happiest of my life. They were fulfilling in a deeply spiritual way. I felt my mind being stretched and it was exhilarating. Traveling had opened my mind and my heart and filled me with energy. My understanding of who I was had fundamentally changed.

As wonderful as my time at Oxford was, it didn't distract me from my intention to become a lawyer. I'd been accepted to law school and was on a legitimate path to success. And yet . . . some part of me, I had to admit, wasn't so sure. "You have always known, ever since you were a little child, that you were here to do something," Litany Burns had told me. "You have a purpose. . . . You are here to help people." Did being a lawyer fit that description? In a way, I guess it did. But was it my true purpose? Was it my best path? The path that would allow me to share my unique gifts with the world?

Right before I graduated, one of my Phi Sigma Sigma sorority sisters, Ann, asked me for a reading. I wasn't particularly close with her; still, she'd heard about my abilities and politely but ur-gently asked for a reading. She didn't want the party trick—she wanted real help. This had never happened to me before. I'd worked hard to keep my psychic encounters with people light and casual. But Ann needed answers.

We sat down at a table in the kitchen of my house. Ann jumped right in.

"I need to know something," she said. "I need to know if I am going to be with my current boyfriend in the future."

Ann had been dating a nice guy for a couple of years. And, like a lot of girls with college boyfriends, she was wondering if she'd found her life partner or if the relationship was as fleeting and finite as college itself. I sensed her concern and anxiety. Sitting across from her, I felt something I hadn't ever felt before while using my abilities. I felt a sense of responsibility.

"I mean, I love him, I really do," Ann went on. "But I need to know if I'm supposed to be with him for life. Can you tell me if we're going to be together forever? Can you tell me that?"

I wasn't sure what information, if any, would come through, and I was relieved when I quickly got an image. I saw Ann in a white dress.

"Yes," I blurted out. "Yes, you will be together. You're going to get married. And you will buy a house, and then you will have kids. More than one kid. Two or three. That is the path you're on together. You are going to make a life with him and you will be happy."

I watched the anxiety disappear from her face. Her face flushed and a big smile lit up her whole being. Calm washed over her, transforming her from the inside out. It was one of the most beautiful, powerful transformations I'd ever witnessed. At a very deep level the reading filled Ann with peace and joy and certainty.

But hers wasn't the only transformation that day. While I read for Ann, I also felt something begin to change inside me. As I said, Ann and I hadn't been especially close. But during the reading and afterward I felt incredibly close to her.

Something about the exchange we were having—me receiving her energy, interpreting it, and sending it back to her as specific, meaningful details—forged a connection between us. There was no judgment, no weird sense of invasion, no feeling that this was frivolous, only a feeling of love and connectedness and purpose. For the first time, I felt like I'd been invited into something profound and meaningful, something bigger than Ann or me. I felt authority; I took ownership of my gift.

Ann did go on to marry her boyfriend, and they had children. Last I heard, they were still happy on their journey through life together.

9

Sedona

I SHOULD HAVE FELT EXCITED about graduating, but, strangely, it felt anticlimactic. My family came up for the ceremony, and that was wonderful, but to me the whole thing seemed unnecessary. Graduation didn't feel like a chapter of my life coming to a close; it felt like an expansion.

At the graduation ceremony I felt saturated and off-balance and vulnerable as I took in the collective energy of everyone's elation, mixed with a strong current of anxiety and sadness. This torrent of emotion, radiating out from thousands of people, was overwhelming. I'd never been in such a large crowd where everyone's feelings were so lined up and so powerful, and I felt knocked over by a tremendous shift in the energy around me. It wasn't a good feeling.

I realized I needed a way to protect myself from other people's energy and emotions. I'd been struggling with this for years, but now that I was going out into the world, the task took on more urgency. I focused intently on how I could block out other people's energy and not feel saturated. I needed a shield. I began picturing a kind of force field around my body. I'd picture a white light coming down over my head, encapsulating my body, and sealing off my energy as it went into the floor. I felt protected.

After graduation, my friend Gwen and I went on a long-planned trip to Arizona. We landed in Phoenix, rented a red convertible, and drove to Sedona with the top down. The vast, otherworldly sandstone formations—the famous red rocks—changed color from deep red to blistering amber depending on the light. The sights and smells and energy were intoxicating. Sedona made my spirit soar.

On the first day there, we went to a local store that sold crystals. Instantly I was drawn to something on the front counter. It wasn't a crystal or an amulet—it was a business card. I picked it up and read it: *Ron Elgas, Psychic.*

Gwen and I booked appointments. My session with Litany Burns had been momentous, but I was curious to see if her insights were specific to me or if everyone who went to a psychic got a similar reading. After our readings, Gwen and I would compare notes.

Ron's wife greeted us at the door to their house in overalls and braids, and welcomed us in with a big smile. The house was airy and filled with a lovely light. When Ron entered the room, his energy hit me right away. It was warm and comforting. He wore his pale hair in a ponytail, and his face was friendly and relaxed. Ron sat in a chair, while I sat on the sofa across from him.

The reading began. Ron looked at me, and the first words out of his mouth were, "Bright energy." Then he took a long pause.

"You hold your energy in a certain way," he finally said. "It's called God fire. It has to do with your commitment to your higher self. Whatever you do in your life, it will still have to do with the spirit. Whatever lessons you need to learn along the way to your ultimate path, you will learn them."

Ron went on. "All this light and energy around you, when I see it, it's not normal. They show me beams of light shooting out of your body in all directions. There is a connection to the infinite spirit, and that connection is prewired in you. It's a choice you already made. It's your destiny."

What is my destiny? I thought. *What does all that mean?*

"I see you are linked to a large consortium of individuals— a consortium of light beings," Ron explained. "They work *through* you. They can run power through you. There is a gigantic power grid all around you that you are connected to. I don't know how you are going to use it, but it is your destiny. You're going to create a lot of change and awakenings around you."

Ron went on to tell me more about myself. He took long pauses, as if listening intently, then spoke quickly and surely. He could see I was still uncomfortable accessing information about people, and he gave me a helpful tip. "Don't try so hard to hear it," Ron said. "It will come easily to you. When you see something or hear something, don't act scared or uncertain. Just do what you do, and you will have results." Ron told me that whatever my true purpose was, I wasn't going to find it right away. I would open up to it, then retreat. Open up, retreat. It would be a struggle. He also saw me getting married and having three kids—two girls and a boy. That would all happen before I fully embraced my true path.

And then, one day, "you will find yourself in front of people," Ron said. "Teaching, speaking . . . spiritual things. You will open doors energetically for others. You will do something similar to what I do. You will shift people's energy because you are here to help people reach higher levels of consciousness. You will teach people and help people to see that level. You will do other things first—you will have a family, do other things. But there will be an expansion going on in you—a connecting of links that will move you into your destiny. And then you will step into your destiny. You will help teach humanity."

Teaching again. I couldn't get away from it.

"You are still looking and searching," Ron continued. "You haven't quite got it yet. You haven't found what you want. But it is there. It is not outside you, it's inside you. The entire universe is *inside you*. Be quiet and listen to yourself, and very gently move around in that energy. I don't know when you're going to find it, but it's already there. Laura, you have a mission."

Afterward, in the car, I asked Gwen about her reading. Her reading had been nothing like mine. They hadn't talked about light or destiny or a connection to higher spiritual beings. Her reading had been more concrete, more about challenges she'd face and her immediate road ahead.

Gwen and I soaked up as much of the beauty and power of Sedona as we could. We meditated in the canyons with a shaman and swam in a river near a natural rockslide. Then it was off to the Grand Canyon. When we got there we stepped out of our car, looked around, and said, "Eh." The grandeur of the canyon was no match for the incredible energy and pull of Sedona. The next day we jumped in the convertible and drove straight back to Sedona.

Back in New York, it was time to send in the deposit for law school to secure my enrollment in the fall. I held the letter in my hands for a long while. It all felt wrong.

Something was changing. It had started with Litany Burns, then continued with Arlene and Ron. It had been spurred on by Professor Bosnick, then Oxford, then Sedona. I wasn't at a starting point, as I had thought—I was at a crossroads. Deep down, I already knew which path I had to choose.

I found my mother in the kitchen.

"Mom, I don't want to go to law school," I said. "I want to teach."

My mother looked up and smiled. There was something knowing in her smile. Then she came over and hugged me.

"Well," she said simply. "That's wonderful."

At the age of twenty-two, I earned a master's in teaching secondary-school English.

While I applied for teaching positions, I worked in the education department of a nonprofit. I was seeing a guy named Sean, and we were in love. He was a musician with a beautiful, artistic, passionate energy. Listening to him sing and play songs he'd written filled me with joy. We moved into a converted garage in Huntington Village on Long Island. It had a big, drafty living area, with a small bathroom and shower attached to a room in the back. It had a nook of a kitchen and a tiny partitioned bedroom. To me, it was heaven.

I had a boyfriend, a master's degree, my own cozy apartment, and even a little terrier named Quincy. It was everything I'd hoped for. Finally my life was making sense. I felt more connected to my abilities and less anxious about them.

I took out an ad in the local *Pennysaver*:

PSYCHIC READINGS
CALL LAURA

10

Disturbance

THE FIRST PERSON to answer my ad was an older woman who lived in Lloyd Neck, not too far from where I grew up. Her name was Delores. We arranged a day and time to meet, and I gave her my address. The day of the reading, I was so nervous I had trouble catching my breath. I'd never done a formal reading with someone who wasn't a friend or acquaintance, and I had no plan or protocol in place. I didn't really even know what a reading was. What if my gift failed me?

The doorbell rang. There was no turning back. I opened the door and saw Delores standing there, every bit as nervous as I was. She was hunched and closed off and she seemed small. I led her inside and we sat at the kitchen table. The lights were low, and I'd lit a candle. She looked at me with sad, imploring eyes. I wasn't sure how to begin.

Luckily, Delores started for me, telling me why she was there.

"I'm sixty years old and I want to adopt a child," she said. "I believe it is the right thing for me, but I want to know for sure."

Anyone sitting across from this woman could tell she was lonely and somehow broken. But I knew something else about her—I understood that her husband had recently passed. I knew it because I saw him, or rather a bright point of light that I knew to be him, in the field of vision just above my eyes. And I could tell he was someplace else. I knew he was not with her.

As soon as I understood this, more information about Delores came through. I could see she was completely lost without her husband and desperately clutching for some kind of support, direction, comfort. She was off-balance, confused, and aimless, and she didn't know where to go or what to do.

Most clearly, though, what came through was her pain. A searing, soul-deep pain. The kind of pain that cripples and confuses us—pain that demands an answer. I felt the pain, just as I'd felt other people's pain and sadness for much of my life. Only now it was even more intense, more focused. Now I was inviting it in.

And as I felt it, I also understood what Delores was trying to do. For her, the way to answer her pain was to bring someone new into her life. She wanted to adopt a child in order to fill the horrible void left by her husband's passing, not because of a desire to nurture and mentor a young soul.

What was even clearer to me was that adopting a child, at her age and in her situation, would be a terrible mistake. That certainty wasn't coming from me. It was being told to me. Adoption wasn't meant to be her path.

Before I figured out what I wanted to say, I found I was already talking. The words just tumbled out. I don't remember formulating thoughts or arranging ideas—it was more of a stream of insight. It almost felt like I was translating for someone else.

"You cannot make the mistake of tangling your path with

someone else's," I said. "You can't fill up the space inside you with someone else. You need to confront your loneliness. And you have to find another way to feel connected to the universe again. There is another path for you to follow. You can join a reading group, meet new people, bring an animal into your life—an animal that needs your love and protection and comfort. An animal that is meant to cross paths with you."

Delores listened intently. Only later did it occur to me that my debut as a professional psychic was telling a lonely older woman to get a pet.

The reading went on for about an hour. After she left, I tried to gauge what, if any, impact I'd had on her. From what I could tell she seemed relieved—not as tense, less heavy, like something inside her had lifted. Perhaps she already knew adopting would be a bad idea, if not impossible, and only needed to hear it from someone else. It was hard for me to conclude I'd actually helped Delores in any real way. But I believed that what I'd told her was real and true and meaningful. I never spoke with her again, so I cannot say if my first professional reading was a success or a failure.

But I felt good enough about it to keep going.

The responses to my ad kept coming in. Many more than I'd expected—dozens of them. I even got a call from a woman in Virginia, asking if I'd read her over the phone.

"I don't know," I said. "I've never tried it."

"Well, can you try it and we'll see what happens?"

And so I did my first telephone reading. Once again, I had no protocol in place, no system, no structure. I was winging it. But to my great surprise and relief, the phone reading worked. As much information came through as if we'd been sitting side by side.

A few weeks later I got a call from a man named Paul. Paul was anxious for a reading, and we made an appointment. He showed up at my apartment and took a seat at the kitchen table. He was in his late twenties, and overall, his energy seemed cheerful and confident, even though he was a little nervous that day. I started getting various bits of information right away, and a lot of it was about his girlfriend, Amy, whom he clearly loved a lot. Almost immediately the reading and the information I was getting focused mainly on her and Paul's relationship with her.

But then something happened. For the first time in a reading, I felt a presence somewhere behind me, and to my right. Before then, everything had always seemed to be right in front of me. I hadn't really pinpointed where, specifically, I was seeing the information, but it never felt like it was behind me. It was more like when you get a thought in your head—it doesn't pop in from the right side or the left side, it's just there.

But now I realized my field of vision was bigger and broader than I'd thought. There was more than one direction for information to come to me—there was a new, distinctly different portal that was open. And what came through on my right side, slightly behind me, then moving in front, was clear and vivid—a strong, forceful presence. I heard a name. Who was this? What was happening? I didn't know. I just let what I was seeing and hearing tumble out.

"I am getting someone named Chris connected to Amy," I told Paul. "I'm being given details about Amy."

I was astonished by how specific the details were. Amy's shoe size, the purse she liked, her favorite hat, other intimate things. Paul listened quietly as I kept the details coming. But the more I spoke, the more confused I got—why was Paul's reading about Amy and not about him? I began to feel uncomfortable for him, and after a while I forced myself to stop.

"Paul, I'm really sorry, I know this isn't what you came here to hear," I said. "I don't know why your reading is all about Amy and Chris."

"It's okay," Paul said calmly. He didn't seem upset or offended. "Everything you're telling me is a hundred percent accurate. Everything you're saying is true."

I was relieved to hear that, but it still didn't explain what was going on. Paul took a deep breath and explained it to me.

"Chris is dead," he said softly. "He died in a car crash when he was dating Amy. She was with him in the car when it crashed."

I felt a chill run through my body. What was Paul telling me? That Chris was coming to me from the beyond? That I was hearing from a dead person as clearly as if he were right in my apartment?

At that moment, I felt awe. I was coming to grips with my ability as a psychic, the ability to perceive a person's soul energy and life path. But I'd never considered that I might also be a medium, someone who is able to communicate with the Other Side. And yet in that reading I was getting clear, specific details from someone who had crossed. I didn't have to root around for it or struggle to pull it out—it just came through, like water through an open tap.

I reacted with fear. *This is a deal breaker,* I thought. *This is too weird. This is too much responsibility. I'm not ready for this.*

I was only twenty-three, not at all equipped to handle this kind of responsibility. I didn't understand what it meant to communicate with someone who had passed—I was frightened by it. I didn't see any beauty or grace in it; instead it felt weird and wrong. All the old, negative feelings about my gift suddenly came back.

With Paul's permission, I continued the reading. Chris was there and he was insistent, wanting to focus on Amy. The information that came through was that she and Paul were meant to be together. They were meant to grow together on their paths.

They would eventually get married, and they would have two children.

When the reading was over I said goodbye to Paul and wished him well. He seemed happy with the information I gave him, not at all spooked that his girlfriend's dead boyfriend was watching over them.

But I was left reeling. I wondered how the reading would affect my path going forward, now that I could connect with people who had crossed. What I didn't yet fully understand was that I wasn't just responsible for conveying information from the Other Side. I was also responsible for *interpreting* it.

Looking back now, I can see what Chris was trying to do. He was trying to give Paul his blessing. He was validating his own connection to Paul's girlfriend, and in so doing making it clear he wished her great love and happiness with Paul. Chris did not hurl himself through the portal and hijack Paul's reading to make him jealous or complicate his relationship—the Other Side does not deal in negativity. Everything that comes through from the Other Side, I would come to learn, is based in love.

But I didn't know any of that back then. All I knew was that my reading with Paul frightened me. That night I told Sean about the experience.

"I don't understand what happened," I said. "I don't think I'm okay with it. I'm not sure I want to do this anymore."

Yet people kept calling. My ad wasn't even running anymore, but people were hearing about me from friends, and they all wanted a reading. One evening I heard a knock on the front door, but when I opened it no one was there. There was only a note taped to the door.

"I need to talk to you," the note read. "I need a reading. Please call me."

I shut the door, then crumpled up the note and threw it away. I felt invaded and vulnerable. I wasn't ready for this responsibility.

On the night of July 17, 1996, I was home alone. Sean was at work, due back soon. I was relaxing, reading a book. It was an unremarkable evening. But then, sometime after 8:00 p.m., my body involuntarily twitched and tensed.

I sat upright and braced myself against a sudden onrush of dread. This wasn't like the waves of sadness that sometimes washed over me when I was near sad people—this was a deep, existential feeling of horror and chaos and disruption, as if the world were ending. I didn't know what it was or what was causing it, but I knew something terrible had occurred. I knew there had been a disturbance in the universe—and it was a horrible, wretched, paralyzing thing to know. Suddenly I felt like I couldn't breathe. In a panic, I called Sean.

"Is everything okay?" I asked him through gulps for air.

"Yes, everything's fine," he said.

But nothing felt fine to me. My voice lilted into a high pitch as I fought back tears that were choking my speech. "*Please* come home," I begged him, "and please drive carefully. I need you here. Something is wrong."

I turned on the TV while I waited for him, and a special news bulletin flashed on the screen. Something about an airplane, a crash. Video of fiery streaks across a black sky. I sat down and tried to clear my head so I could pay attention. But I already knew everything I needed to know.

There had been a tragedy, and the tragedy had been made known to me.

By the time Sean pulled into the driveway, I was a sobbing mess. "What's wrong with me?" I asked him. "Why do I have to feel these things? Why do I have to know but not be able to change the outcome? Why do I have these abilities?"

A familiar feeling came over me—a feeling of being cursed.

The awful details emerged over the next few days. TWA Flight

800, a Boeing 747-100 flying from New York's JFK Airport to Rome, exploded in the night sky and crashed into the Atlantic Ocean near East Moriches on Long Island. The explosion and crash happened about forty miles away from where I lived. All 230 people on board the flight were killed.

The horror of the crash and my awareness of a disturbance before I heard about it were devastating. That event wiped out all the progress I'd been making in coming to terms with my gift. Once again, I simply did not want to have this knowledge. I was frightened that I was able to hear people who had died and asked to deliver their messages. It was too great a responsibility. So I stopped. I stopped taking calls. I stopped answering knocks on the door. I stopped thinking of myself as a psychic. I vowed never to do a reading again.

It all went away, the calls and the knocks and the readings, and I tried to live my life as a normal person. The universe left me alone for a while. The Other Side quit coming through, and my mysterious field of vision went dark, as if whatever forces were guiding me decided to leave me be. I wasn't ready.

PART TWO

11

Staying Open

A FEW MONTHS AFTER I stopped doing readings, I got my
first teaching job. The high school was only a half hour from
where I'd grown up, but the neighborhood couldn't have been
more different. It was plagued by drugs and crime. At the school,
security guards patrolled the halls. Most of the students came
from broken homes. Many had only one parent. Some had only
an uncle or an aunt. Some didn't even have that.

My first day in the classroom, I quickly saw how tough it would
be. The students were distracted and defiant. In one senior English class, right in the middle of my lesson, a girl named Yvette
got up from her seat, walked to the window, opened it, and spat.
Then she sauntered back to her chair. The entire class turned and
looked at me, waiting for my reaction.

I let it go. I let it go because I knew why Yvette had done what
she did. She hadn't done it to challenge me. She'd done it to get
my attention.

My ability to read people's energies allowed me to understand what was really going on with the students. They weren't bad kids—they were needy kids. They craved attention and care and love. They were lost, confused, and desperate for guidance, but to protect themselves they acted mean and tough. They were used to not being seen for who they really were.

I could feel their anger and frustration; I could see their energies being blocked. Most of all, I could read their pain—it hung over them like a dark cloud. They didn't have what they needed to be good students. They needed love.

Not reacting when Yvette spat out the window would be a defining moment for me as a teacher. I knew it could backfire—the students might see me as someone they could walk all over. But I had to follow my instinct, and my instinct wasn't to get angry. It was to dive into their pain.

After class, I walked over to Yvette.

"Honey, are you okay?" I asked. "Are you not feeling well?"

Yvette seemed stunned.

"I'm okay," she said softly, and then she shuffled away.

After that, Yvette began to open up to me a little more every day. We talked about her life, and I helped her with her studies. The connection between us deepened. She didn't have to pretend around me, and she didn't have to work to get my attention, because she already had it.

In that first exchange with Yvette, my teaching philosophy was born. I loved books and I loved learning, but I also loved kids. Teaching wasn't just about preparing students for tests; it was about connecting with them and helping them see their own light and reach their full potential. It was about making them know they mattered in this world.

I wanted them to know that their insights and energy mattered in the classroom, too. If a student cut my class, I'd have someone watch the class, and then I'd head to the cafeteria and find the cutter. "Hey!" I'd say. "Come on, you need to come to class. It'll be exciting!" At first they'd look at me like I was crazy, but then they would follow me to class. They weren't angered or annoyed; they were happy! They were happy because someone cared about them.

At the end of that semester, Yvette came up to me and handed me a card she'd made. It had heart stickers on it. She'd written, "Thank you so much. I will miss you and always remember you."

Yvette's note wiped away any lingering uncertainty about my decision not to pursue a career in law.

I was a teacher. Teaching was my path.

By now, Sean and I had been together for about a year. We were in love. He'd proposed to me, and I'd said yes. But even so, I felt uneasy about our relationship. The night Sean and I got engaged, I had a vivid, 3-D dream that the diamond on my finger was made of sugar and that I'd washed my hands and watched it dissolve under the stream of water. I woke up knowing what it meant, but I just wasn't ready to admit it.

We were on completely different schedules, too. I'd get up at 5:00 a.m. to get ready for school, while many nights Sean would stay out till 4:00 a.m. playing with his band. We saw each other less and we argued more. After a while, an image formed in my head. I could see myself on a rowboat drifting away from shore— drifting away from Sean. Either I could start rowing back to him or I could simply paddle away.

I chose to paddle away.

I moved out of our garage apartment and back in with my parents. The breakup was painful. I was heartbroken and retreated into myself. When I wasn't teaching, I was reading, writing poetry, and hanging out at the local bookstore.

My friend Jill called me one night and said, "Laura, you need to join the world again."

She had a proposition—she wanted me to go out with her, her boyfriend Chris, and one of Chris's buddies.

"Not interested," I said.

"Laura, you have to go," she said. "Just come along, you'll have fun."

"Seriously, no thanks," I said. "The last thing I need is to be set up on a date."

Jill was insistent. "It's not a setup. It's just a bunch of friends having a good time."

"It sounds like a blind date to me."

"Okay, how about this," Jill said. "I'll ask Chris to bring two friends. That way it won't be just you and one guy."

I thought about it. As long as it wasn't a blind date, what was the harm? The worst thing that could happen was I'd have a lousy time.

"Okay," I said. "But make sure he brings two guys."

A few days later I took the train into Manhattan with Jill and Chris. I felt moody and regretted that I'd agreed to come.

We met Chris's friends by the Long Island Railroad waiting room. One of them was a short, outgoing fellow named Rich, who pounced on me and wouldn't leave me alone for the rest of the night. The other guy was tall and reserved. Chris introduced us, and when we shook hands something inside me changed.

It was sharp and sudden, like having my fingers beneath a faucet that quickly turned from cold to hot. I can't say it was romantic; it wasn't even really a feeling. I heard an inner voice cut through the clamor of Penn Station, and it said, *Be open.*

Those two words were enough to neutralize my negative thoughts. *You don't have to do anything,* I thought. *All you have to do is be open.*

"Hi," he said. "I'm Garrett."

I didn't know anything about him, other than that he was going to law school in Brooklyn. For most of the evening we didn't get much of a chance to talk to each other, because Rich wouldn't leave my side. Around midnight we decided to go to one last bar. It was a tiny place, dark and smoky, with just a few tables in the back. When Rich excused himself to go to the restroom, Garrett and I found ourselves sitting next to each other.

"So," Garrett said casually, "what's your story?"

I told Garrett my story. My whole story.

I spilled my guts to him in that smoky little bar. I told him about my childhood, my fears, my recent breakup. No spin, no sugarcoating, just everything. Garrett matched my honesty. He told me how painful his parents' divorce had been for him. He told me that his last relationship had ended badly just a few months earlier. We told each other things no one on a quasi blind date would ever dream of sharing.

When it was time to head home, Garrett asked for my phone number.

On our first official date, at a fancy seafood restaurant in Manhattan, I fell right back into the pattern of spilling my guts. There was no artifice, no pretense—nothing to get in our way. I worked up the nerve to tell Garrett about my abilities. He was curious, maybe even fascinated, but not at all fazed.

There was no real courtship period. Within four months of meeting, we were talking about marriage.

12

The Arrival

IT HAPPENED ON a warm summer Sunday, in the skies above New York's Jones Beach.

Garrett worked full-time and was putting himself through law school at night. His hours were crazy. Between work and classes and studying he didn't have much time to spend with me. About a year into our relationship, I was at Jones Beach with my mother. My brother was competing in the Jones Beach Triathlon and we were there to cheer him on. I've always found Jones Beach, located on one of the slender barrier islands off the southern coast of Long Island, to be a wonderful, spiritual place. Looking out on the endless horizon, I feel connected to the universe.

But on that day, I felt something blot out the sun. I looked up and saw a dark, shimmering curtain draw itself across the sky. When my eyes adjusted I could tell it wasn't black at all—it was a rich, radiant amber. And it was moving, fluttering, alive somehow, letting through little shafts of sunlight and sweeping across the length of the beach. I stood in the sand transfixed, in awe of this rare and powerful thing in the air.

As I stared at it I realized it wasn't one thing but thousands of things—tens of thousands of monarch butterflies.

We were witnessing a migration. Great swarms of monarchs, their bright orange wings ringed in black, making their brave journey from Canada to Mexico, ahead of the winter cold that could kill them. They seemed to fill every inch of the sky, some of them daring to flitter down and land on an arm or a shoulder before peeling away and rejoining the flight. It was magical. I felt an overwhelming love and affection for the butterflies, not just because this was such an unexpected thrill but because for me it was a sign. When I was little my grandfather had a brown and white butterfly that always "visited" him when he sat outside on the porch. After he died, a brown and white butterfly would "visit" my family from time to time. We called it Pop Pop's butterfly. When I was older, I decided to ask my guides and loved ones on the Other Side for a sign of my own so I could know they were around. I chose a monarch butterfly because orange is my favorite color. Without fail, monarch butterflies would appear before a big test or an important choice, to let me know they were there for me and that I wasn't alone.

And now, quite literally out of the blue, here they were! I turned to my mother and grabbed her by the arm.

"This is it," I said. "The universe is telling me something. The monarchs are celebrating! Something miraculous is going to happen!"

I watched the monarchs for as long as I could, until they were just a smudge in the distant sky. What were they announcing? I wondered. What was the universe trying to tell me?

The next day, I learned I was pregnant.

The instant I found out I was pregnant, everything made sense. In that instant I felt an overwhelming, overpowering, unconditional love for my unborn child.

The feeling was deep and unshakable. I felt connected to something so much bigger and more meaningful than my little life. I was part of something vast and wonderful and miraculous. I was now the doorway for a new life to enter the world! I felt honored and at peace. My child would be raised with love, and she would grow up to be brave and strong, and she would change the world! Suddenly it didn't matter that Garrett and I sometimes fought. We were fighting because we still had to grow and change and improve. But we were meant to grow and change and improve together. It would be hard work, but we would help each other become the people—and the parents—we were meant to be. This wasn't just my path. This was our path.

We got married in a Lutheran church on Long Island and settled comfortably into married life. Three weeks before my due date, I went into labor. In a delivery room at Huntington Hospital, our beautiful daughter arrived.

Her name was Ashley.

She was so tiny and so pink and pudgy, and her little eyes were swollen shut. As I held her I didn't feel like I was meeting her for the first time—I felt like I already knew her, as if she had always been a part of me. And now that she was here, I felt my soul energy double. I felt larger than who I was. My unconditional love for Ashley was already changing me—I was growing and graduating to some other level. Because of the miracle of Ashley, my life would never be the same.

The crash of TWA Flight 800 had put an end to my psychic readings, and for almost three years I'd shut down my gift. I still read people's energies—I couldn't not do that—but the portal to the Other Side was closed.

However, a few days before I learned I was pregnant, I started feeling a strange energy. Sometimes I felt so much energy I had to lace up my sneakers and go for a run. I felt like I was back in my soccer-playing days, when the only thing that could calm me down was hours of nonstop running. I didn't know where all this energy was coming from. I just went for long runs until I burned it off.

But after discovering I was pregnant, my energy grew even more intense. I also started getting flashes of information—words, images, noises, scenes—just as I did during readings. That continued throughout my pregnancy, but after Ashley was born, I tried not to think about it, and I carried on with my normal life. I wasn't interested in letting the Other Side back in.

I soon realized what was happening. Ashley's birth had opened a portal of light between the world she came from and this world. And once that portal was open, there was no way to close it. The Other Side rushed through. Ashley's arrival filled me with a great, powerful love—and made me feel connected to humanity in a beautiful and profound way.

One morning before work I told Garrett, "I think I have to start doing readings again."

I was a newlywed and a brand-new mom. I'd also gotten a tenure-track position at a new high school. Garrett was working full-time and going to law school at night. Why would I want to open the door to the Other Side again and let all that into our busy lives? I had no choice.

"You could be jeopardizing your teaching job," Garrett said.

"Then I'll do it anonymously," I said. I simply couldn't turn off the flood of information I was getting. I couldn't ignore the pull.

This time I put a listing on eBay. I used only my middle name, Lynne, and I called myself a clairvoyant. I put down $5 as the opening bid for a reading. I didn't know if anyone would bite. But within a day several people made bids. The final price was $75. It came from a middle-aged police officer in Arizona. We set up a time to talk.

On the day of the reading I felt all the familiar anxiety. I wasn't sure if anyone or anything would come through.

I called the police officer at the appointed time, and right away two figures came through—his mother and father. They were there to reassure and comfort their son. They let him know they were okay and at peace and proud of him. His mother spoke about all he had done for her before she crossed. His father indicated that he had crossed from a heart attack and they hadn't had a chance to say goodbye. They told him to let go of his guilt for the things he'd left unsaid. By the end of the reading the officer's voice had changed. He sounded relieved, even happy. I understood that the reading had been a profoundly healing event for him. When we hung up, I was exhausted and exhilarated.

Ashley hadn't just opened a door; she'd blown it wide open.

———

I was aware that Garrett wasn't altogether comfortable with what I was doing. He had always been open to my gift and supportive, but now he was seeing that these readings would be a big part of my life, and he was concerned.

"How do you know you're not connecting to the dark side?" he asked. "How do you know you're not communicating with the devil?"

They were valid questions, and my only answer was that I just knew. I knew because everything that came through in my readings was beautiful and based in love. Still, at this point I hadn't done all that many readings. They felt good and right, but what if they weren't? What exactly was it that I was letting into my home and my family?

I didn't have any good answers.

Then one day I read for a woman who was around my age and who, like me, had a daughter. Except her daughter, Hailey, had passed away at the age of three.

In the reading I felt a crushing sadness and knew this mother was trapped beneath it. There were layers and layers of guilt, because the mother felt she'd let Hailey down by not saving her. She'd become a virtual shut-in, rarely leaving her home, ignoring holidays, avoiding friends, suffering every hour of every day. Her life, her heart, her soul—they were all horribly broken. I was speaking with someone who no longer knew how to live.

Early in the reading, a tiny figure came through. I could tell it was a girl. The child told me all about her mother—how she blamed herself for failing her daughter, how she was frozen in grief. Then she put her hand to her stomach, and I knew what she was trying to convey.

"She is coming through," I told the mother. "She is saying that she passed because of a liver condition. There was nothing you could have done to change that. She is saying she was not meant to be here with us for very long. She was meant to come here and feel unconditional love, but she was not meant to stay. She says you mustn't confuse sadness with guilt. You must let go of the guilt. You feel you failed her as a mother because you couldn't save her. But it wasn't your role to save her. It was your role to love her."

There was a long silence on the other end of the phone, punctuated by small, faint sobs. That this woman's brave, beautiful daughter was coming through and offering comfort—that she was so determined to help her mother heal—was incredibly moving not just for her mother but for me as well.

A few days later, I got a package from the mother in the mail.

She wrote that our reading had lifted her cloud of misery and allowed her to breathe again. Knowing her daughter was still with her had changed everything. For the first time in a long, long time, she'd been able to leave her house and see friends. Her daughter had saved her life.

Along with the letter there was something carefully packaged in bubble wrap. It was a little ceramic figurine—a tiny angel. The mother explained that she'd bought the angel before her daughter got sick, because it looked like her little girl. After her daughter passed, the ceramic angel had been this woman's most cherished possession—her only link, she believed, to the beautiful soul that had been ripped away.

But now, she wrote, she wanted me to have the angel. She still cherished it, but she said she didn't need it as much anymore.

I showed the letter and the angel to Garrett. He read the letter and then went off on his own. A little while later, he returned and sat down beside me in the living room, the little angel in his hand.

"Your reading changed her life," Garrett said. "She was paralyzed with grief. She was stuck in her home and she didn't want to live, and after speaking with you she wanted to live again. Everything in this letter is pure and positive and beautiful. It is all about healing. What you're doing is all about healing."

Garrett's conviction strengthened mine. After a lifetime of struggling with my gift, I knew now that I was meant to embrace it. I don't know if I could have gotten to that place without Garrett. In the end, we got there together.

13

The Screen

WHEN I FIRST STARTED to do readings, while I was living with Sean, I didn't really understand what a reading was. I knew I could access and read a person's energy, and I knew this gave me bits of information about that person's path and purpose in life. Eventually I realized I could also connect with people who had crossed to the Other Side. I could be a "go-between" for people on earth and those who have crossed. I'd learned it was my responsibility to interpret everything that came through, to be a translator of sorts. At first it was difficult, like learning a foreign language. But over time I got better at it. I began to understand what certain symbols meant. It was like playing—and getting good at—a game of psychic charades.

Even so, I'd never developed a protocol for my readings that allowed me to switch from one gift to another and back again without everything getting confused. But after Ashley was born and the information from the Other Side began to come through more clearly and forcefully, I had to find a more organized way to communicate with the Other Side. Before long, I developed a reading method. Just as I had done with teaching and classroom management, I came up with a system that made connecting with dead people much more efficient.

First, I came to see that I am most comfortable doing readings over the phone because I am able to focus more fully. That's not to say I can't read effectively face-to-face or in front of large groups—it's just that reading remotely over the phone allows me to disappear, as it were, and become an instrument.

I start by going to my bedroom, closing the door, and turning the lights down very low. I sit in a yoga-style position and take off my socks. It may sound silly, but when the soles of my bare feet touch it seems to create a loop so that energy can flow continuously through my body.

I close my eyes and focus on my breathing. Once I feel ready, I slip on my cordless headset and contact the person I'm reading— the sitter. Then I close my eyes again. My eyes stay closed the entire time I'm reading, opening only when I feel the energy of the Other Side pulling back and my own energy shifting.

When the sitter is on the call, I say a few words about what I'm going to do and what role the sitter will play in the reading. I explain that when I read, I think of it as a triangle of light—my energy plugging into the sitter's energy and the energy of his or her loved one on the Other Side. I also ask the sitter to hold any questions until the end of the reading, because it is my hope that the Other Side will address in the course of the reading what the sitter wants to know. I explain how a reading is like a game of psychic charades. Words, numbers, names, dates, symbols, images—all sort of things come through. It's my job to interpret the information and pass it on. I'll tell the sitter that if I say something that doesn't make sense, he or she shouldn't try to make it fit but rather should tell me it doesn't resonate.

For example, the Other Side may show me a giant apple to indicate to me that the sitter is a teacher. But I might misinterpret that and say, "Do you love to bake apple pies?" If the sitter tells me that doesn't make sense, I'll take a step back and try to reinterpret the image. But if the sitter is being polite and tries to make it fit, I may miss the message. I also tell the sitter that as long as he or she understands the message I'm bringing through, it is fine if I don't. This happens quite often. The sitter's loved one will pass along a message and the sitter will understand exactly what it means, but it doesn't make sense to me. Later, at the end of a reading or in an email, the sitter may tell me what the message meant, and it's usually something very specific or even an inside joke. It always amazes me how the Other Side manages to pass such intimate messages though me without me being aware of their meaning.

During the reading, once I am fully connected, a field of vision emerges. A blank rectangular field appears in my mind—an area I call my screen. Not coincidentally, my screen looks a lot like a teacher's blackboard. It's something I shaped and organized to help communicate with the Other Side. Pictures, symbols, images, and even brief film clips appear on my screen.

With practice, I was able to divide the screen in half. On the left side psychic activity occurs. This is where I always start a reading, because it helps me to align and link my energy with the sitter's. It is where I see the sitter's core aura, the color map of his or her soul path. For example, if someone's core color is orange, I know that the person is marked as an artist and that his or her path involves creating art and being filled with art. Blue indicates an advanced soul who is deeply intuitive and is here as a healer and a teacher.

Often I will see more than one color in a sitter's core aura. I also might see a separate, second, more immediate aura that pertains to the sitter's current path. This second aura appears in a line and gives me a quick snapshot of what energy the sitter is coming out of and what energy he or she is currently in. They also give me a map of what lies ahead for the sitter. For example, if I see the color yellow to the left on my screen, followed by green in the middle and then orange to the right, I know it means that person has come out of a period of illness, depression, and low energy, is in the midst of change and growth, and will be going into a highly creative and fruitful period.

The left side of the screen is also where the sitter's spirit guides appear as points of light. Spirit guides are evolved spiritual beings who act as mentors and help guide us on our paths here. We all have them, usually in teams of two or three.

The left side also shows me a horizontal timeline of the sitter's life. These timelines look just like historical timelines, with little vertical lines drawn at certain ages to mark significant events on the sitter's life path, both in the past and in the future.

I stay on the left-hand side of the screen—reading auras, assessing energy, examining timelines—until I see and feel someone "pushing in" on my right-hand screen. The right half of the screen is further divided into top, middle, and lower levels, and these tiers are where I see small but vibrant points of light. These lights are the energy of our visitors from the Other Side. I reserve the upper right part of the screen for loved ones from the mother's side and the lower right for those from the father's side. Friends, cousins, and peers generally appear closer to the middle of the screen.

Once the points of light show up, they will often show me letters, words, names, and images. I will pluck out these clues, determine where they came from, interpret them as best I can, and pass them on to the sitter. I can also "hear" things from the visitors—which is called clairaudience—but this hearing isn't outside my body, it's within. It's the same way you "hear" a thought.

In addition to my screen, the Other Side also uses my physical body to convey information. This is called clairsentience. During a reading I can actually feel things—pressure, congestion, pain. I might feel a heaviness on my chest, as if someone is sitting on me, or I might feel a shortness of breath, a sudden jolt to my chest, or a burning sensation. I might smell smoke, feel warmth, or experience dozens of other sensations—all of which I decode to correspond to specific situations. I can tell which sensation the Other Side will use to convey a heart attack (the sudden jolt) and which is used to convey longer-term heart failure (the sensation of my lungs filling up with fluid).

These feelings are part of the vocabulary of a reading. Maybe it's the teacher in me, but this system of communication helps keep my readings neat and efficient. Without it, I'd be at the mercy of souls who can be as unruly as high school kids on a Friday afternoon. And even with my organized system in place, sometimes they still are! I tell sitters that every reading is different, because everyone's friends and relatives on the Other Side are different. During some readings loved ones on the Other Side will go one at a time, share what they want to say, and then let the next one talk. Other times it's like a psychic free-for-all, with everyone interrupting and talking over each other. No matter how they come through, they always seem happy to have my attention—and the sitter's attention.

You might wonder how those on the Other Side know to use my screen or my body, or even how they find me. My answer: they just know. We are tied to all those we've ever loved by cords of light. Those cords can never be broken. Think of them like a fishing line of love. If you tug on one end, the other end feels the tug. And those on the Other Side are always on the lookout for openings between the worlds. They can locate the portal they need.

The most important thing for a sitter to know is that he or she doesn't need a psychic medium to communicate with loved ones who have passed. If we open our minds and our hearts, we will begin to see the signs and messages they send for us to feel their presence in our everyday lives.

14

To Love and Forgive

ONCE I ESTABLISHED my system of communicating with the Other Side, my readings became clearer and more powerful. One such reading was with a middle-aged woman named Joann. She learned about me from a friend and contacted me for a reading. She had never had a reading before.

Once we got on the phone, Joann's father came through right away. He told me that he had crossed thirty years before. He had committed suicide. He apologized to Joann and explained he hadn't been of clear mind when he crossed. Joann told me that she knew this was true, and that she had understood and forgiven her father years ago.

Then her father showed me a small creature, a tiny kitten. The kitten was with him, by his feet. Joann's father told me it was important for his daughter to know this.

"Joann, this may sound odd," I said, "but your dad is showing

me a kitten there with him and he's telling me it is really important that you know the kitten is okay."

Joann was quiet. It was a few moments before she spoke.

"I know exactly what he's talking about," she said. "I have
never spoken to anyone about this, but I will tell you."

When Joann was a little girl, she'd heard someone say that cats
always land on their feet. She wanted to see for herself if that was
true, so she picked up the family kitten, a tiny thing named Bris-
tle, took her to an open window in the family's fifth-floor apartment, and dropped her out the window. The kitten landed on the
sidewalk and died.

For the next fifty years Joann harbored a deep, wrenching guilt
for what she'd done. She was never able to shake the belief that
deep down she was a horrible person. She never forgave herself
for killing the kitten, and because of that her life was harder and
darker than it ever should have been.

Now, in the reading, her father was coming through and telling her, *Let it go. Put it down. The guilt you're carrying doesn't belong
to you. Forgive yourself and let it go.*

The exchange between Joann and her father was extremely
moving, for Joann and also for me. After the reading Joann began
the process of letting go of her guilt. She spent less time dwelling
on mistakes. Over time she changed this fundamental view of
herself from a horrible, unfeeling person to someone who is kind
and loving and good. She embraced a path of light and became a
clearer, better version of herself.

Our capacity to love and forgive—to accept fallibilities in another and in ourselves—is our greatest strength. The Other Side
showed me that in Joann's reading. It is a crucial lesson for us all,
because love and forgiveness are constants. There will always be
someone in our lives in need of forgiveness. Sometimes that person is you.

Yes, we can carry on in life without forgiveness, and we often do. We'll say, "I'll never forgive him for doing that," and we'll nurse a grievance for years, maybe decades, and sometimes even after the person is gone. Sometimes that inability to forgive follows us when we cross to the Other Side—until we realize our relationships continue past this life and the need for forgiveness never goes away. If we don't learn this lesson, we are prevented from following a true path of light and from becoming our best and truest selves.

But here is the most beautiful news: It is never too late to forgive. And it is never too late to ask for forgiveness.

Joann's reading taught me that everything the Other Side does is done with love. Love is the currency on the Other Side. And if we don't ask for forgiveness, those on the Other Side will find a way to forgive us anyway—just as Joann's father did.

We don't need a reading with a psychic medium to access forgiveness from the Other Side. All you have to do is ask for it. You can reach your loved ones by projecting your thoughts to them. When you project forgiveness to the Other Side, your loved one always gets the message. All you have to do to forgive a lost loved one is to grant that forgiveness, and all we have to do to be forgiven is to ask. Forgiveness—whether we need it or bestow it—is a miraculous gift.

I saw how forgiveness changed Joann's life. Forgiveness healed her.

Another one of my early readings also taught me much about the power of forgiveness. Barb, a woman in her fifties, also had heard about me from a friend. Barb called me from her kitchen in Pennsylvania, and throughout the reading I could hear her relaying some of what I was saying to her husband, Tony, who was nearby.

"He doesn't believe in any of this," Barb told me. "He thinks when you die, that's it—you go in the ground and you're gone.

But I want you to talk to him anyway." Before I could object, she handed the phone to Tony.

Oh, great, I thought. *How is this going to work? Will the Other Side even come through for a skeptic?* Tony gave me a grumpy hello, which was his way of letting me know he wasn't buying any of this. I took a deep breath, waiting for someone to come through for him. And then someone did—his father.

He told me his name was Robert and he had an urgent message for his son.

"Your father is here, and he wants to tell you something very important," I told Tony. "And it's really important that I get this right and say it the right way. Your father wants me to tell you that he is so sorry about the belt."

On the other end of the line, Tony said nothing. I kept going.

"Your father wants you to know that when he crossed to the Other Side and did his life review he understood what you were doing, and he is very sorry for what he did with the belt," I said. "He is asking for your forgiveness. He wants you to forgive him."

I heard Tony quietly begin to weep.

His father showed me more. He showed me an event, in the form of what I call a "movie clip" in my mind. I saw young Tony sitting on his bed, with the door to his bedroom closed. I saw him holding a belt, and I could tell the belt meant a lot to him. I relayed these images to Tony, who composed himself and told me the story—a story he'd never shared with anyone before.

When Tony was seven, he went to a Boy Scout meeting one cold December night. At the meeting, he was given a do-it-yourself leather belt kit. He was excited because he had the great idea of making his dad a belt for Christmas.

At the meeting he worked hard on the belt, carving in designs, creating belt holes, attaching the buckle. Then he brought it home, hidden in his coat pocket, so he could finish it. He went straight to his bedroom and got to work. In his excitement, Tony forgot to take out the garbage, his nightly chore.

It wasn't the first time Tony had forgotten to take out the garbage. His father would get pretty angry, but on that particular night, Tony's dad stormed up to his bedroom and threw open the door, full of rage.

Then he saw the belt. He grabbed it and beat his son with it. The beating was brief, only several seconds, but it damaged something sacred between Tony and his dad.

"I never ended up giving him the belt," Tony said. "I never even told him about it. I never told anyone. But it's made me sad all these years. I always felt like I had let him down in some way."

Tony's father came through again.

"No!" I told Tony. "Your father says to tell you it was he who let *you* down. He says he just didn't understand the situation then. But now he does. And he is so sorry. He is asking for your forgiveness. He wants you to know how much he loves you and what an excellent son you've always been."

I found myself fighting back tears—but not because of this sad story. I'd just seen a beautiful light pass between Tony and his dad. Tony had carried that hurt around with him his whole life, and now I could feel him letting it go. I was witnessing a great healing between a father and son—after the father had died.

"It's okay, Dad!" he said, his voice cracking with deep emotion. "It's okay! Please tell my father it's okay."

"You don't need me to tell him," I said. "You can tell him yourself. He is with you all the time. He is always right there with you. Just say what you need to say. He can hear you."

Tony handed the phone back to his wife. I could hear him in the background.

"It's okay, Dad," Tony said, over and over. "It's okay, it's okay, it's okay."

From this reading I understood that the cords of light that tie us to those we love can never be broken, not even when we cross. They don't even fray; in fact, they can be strengthened. In my readings with Tony and Joann I saw how relationships can grow even after death. Tony's father understood things in a way he hadn't been able to when he was on earth. I saw that our thoughts and our actions matter greatly to those on the Other Side—that we can help them continue to grow with our love and understanding. We have it in our power to heal the ones we love.

15

What Belongs to You

WITH EACH READING, I learned more. Although many people who came to me were at a crossroads in their lives, unsure of which way to go, I understood that it wasn't my role to dispense advice. The Other Side sends us signs and signals that help us make the right decisions for ourselves.

The first time I met Mary Steffey, I knew she was a special soul. She was a foster mother who had cared for disadvantaged children. I'd read her before, but she came for a reading again because she was facing a big decision—whether or not to adopt a little girl named Aly she'd been fostering. As soon as our reading began, Mary got right to the point.

"Will I harm my daughter Mariah by adopting Aly?" she asked.

I didn't get a clear answer. Instead, I saw Mary's aura. It was purple, which told me that she was an advanced soul who was here in this lifetime to help other souls on their paths. But hovering just around Mary's radiant purple aura was a layer of blackness.

"The blackness means that you feel trapped," I told Mary. "It's coating your energy. It does not mean that you will have a bad life. It just means you will have a life that isn't easy."

Then the matter of Aly came into clearer focus.

"The Other Side is pushing Aly away from her biological family," I said. "Aly has already escaped a doorway to death, a doorway caused by neglect. Now, going forward, I see a thread of possibilities. I see many different doorways, different outcomes. There is more than one possible outcome. And there is another family who might take Aly."

From a past reading I knew some of the details of Mary's life. Her lifelong dream had been to be a mother. She became a social worker so she could be around kids—troubled kids, in particular. She got married—her husband, Tandy, is a well driller who also does environmental work—and got pregnant. But four months in, she lost the baby. She tried again, and lost that baby, too. During one pregnancy she woke up in agony and had to be rushed to the hospital.

"You're lucky," a doctor told her. "Another few minutes and you wouldn't have made it." But Mary didn't feel lucky.

In all, she had endured six failed pregnancies.

With a heavy heart, she gave up on her dream of being a mother—even a foster mother. Without a baby of her own, she didn't think she could emotionally handle fostering a child who would likely get sent back to her biological family. That would be too hard. Instead, Mary started a small kennel and surrounded herself with dogs. She realigned her priorities. She forgot about her dream.

Then one morning she woke up feeling sick. Instantly she knew she was pregnant again. The pregnancy was difficult—everything went wrong. Toxemia, high blood pressure, two hospitalizations. For four long months Mary was put on bed rest. But she held out hope. She even picked out a name for her baby girl—Mariah. She was named after Mary's aunt Mimi. "Whenever there was a storm Mimi used to say, 'When the wind blows hard, it's Mariah at the door.' That was the name I wanted for my child."

One week after she turned thirty-nine, with the baby not quite at full term, Mary went into labor. As soon as the baby was born a nurse whisked her away. Mary waited for news of her baby's condition. Was she strong and healthy? Was she at least five or six pounds? Before long, a nurse came back with the news. Mariah wasn't five or six pounds, or even seven pounds.

Mariah was ten pounds six ounces, and she was strong.

The miracle of Mariah's birth gave Mary the strength to revive her other dream—to become a foster mother.

———

"But what about Mariah?" Mary asked me in our reading. "Will adopting Aly harm her?"

"Everything happens for a reason," I said. "Aly will change Mariah in many ways. Not in a negative way, just in difficult ways. But that does not mean it will be a bad thing. It will just be hard. Aly will always present Mariah with challenges, but I can see that Mariah has a remarkable spirit. And no matter what, Mariah's spirit will sing. It will always sing."

Mary began her career as a foster mom by providing respite care, taking children into her rural Pennsylvania home for short periods of time to give their regular foster parents a break. Mary never took in babies and small children; they were easier to place. Mary took teenagers. The teenagers were usually angry and withdrawn, or surly and impossible to handle. No matter how angry a child was, Mary was able to see past the anger and recognize the wound. She could see the good and vulnerable parts of them.

"Teenagers don't know where they belong, where they fit in," she told me. "Especially these kids, who don't have their own families, who were rejected or abandoned or driven away. Sometimes they act like they're bad, but they're not really bad. They're just trying it on for size."

One day Mary got a phone call from a caseworker at Child Protective Services.

"We have a child we're hoping you can take," the caseworker said. "We just need two weeks until we can figure out a permanent solution."

"Where is she now?" Mary asked.

"In an office here. She's barricaded inside."

"Barricaded? Why?"

"Because she bit everyone."

The child was three years old, and her name was Aly. She'd been the victim of horrible abuse. When her family was ruptured by domestic violence, Aly and her mother lived on the street for several months. They stayed in shelters but never for long, because Aly's aggressive behavior always got them kicked out. She was a biter and a puncher and a scratcher, and she once chased a teacher around a classroom growling like an animal.

She also had a disorder that compelled her to eat everything she got her hands on—nails, pens, crayons, even garbage. She was known to grab adults in inappropriate places. She was nearly four years old, yet she didn't speak—not a single word. The caseworkers likened her to a child raised in the woods. Page after page in her stack of case files referred to her as "feral."

"Mary, I have to tell you," the service worker warned, "Aly is one of the worst cases I've ever seen."

It wasn't a good time for Mary to bring another child into her home. She had recently fallen and broken her ankle. She also had her hands full with Mariah, who was seven and had recently been diagnosed with attention deficit disorder and a condition called sensory processing disorder. All kinds of different sensory stimulation—bright lights, loud noises, an unusual seam in her sock—could set Mariah off and make her bounce around the house or become obsessive. Adding a difficult child like Aly to the mix hardly seemed fair to Mariah, to Mary's husband, or even to Mary. She had every excuse in the world to say no.

Instead she said yes.

Mary told me about the first time she laid eyes on Aly. She stood on her front porch with Mariah and watched a blue Jeep Cherokee pull up in front of the house. One of the rear doors swung open and a caseworker emerged, carrying a child with wild, curly blond hair in her arms. The little girl wore scuffed sneakers that were clearly too small for her, an oversized dirty white T-shirt, and a raggedy pair of shorts. The child looked to be asleep; more likely she'd been sedated.

The caseworker carried Aly to the porch and laid her on a wicker chair. Mary asked if she had any other clothes.

"No, this is it," the caseworker said.

Slowly Aly opened her eyes. Her expression was blank.

"She looks like a war victim," Mariah whispered.

Mary watched the caseworkers drive away. Aly was her problem now. She gathered her courage and took a step toward the child. Aly looked up at her with dull, vacant eyes.

"Hello, Aly," Mary said. "This is my daughter, Mariah."

Mariah gave a little wave. Aly had no reaction. Then Mary said, "And I am . . ."

But before she could finish—before she could even say her name—Aly did something strange. She raised her right hand, stuck out her index finger, put the finger against her temple, and pointed it directly at Mary.

Then Aly said, "Mom."

Nothing in Mary's life had prepared her for Aly, for how wild and angry and disruptive and unpredictable and silent—always hauntingly silent—she could be.

The first time Mary took Aly for a drive, Aly grabbed the metal seatbelt buckle and smashed it into Mariah's face. A few days later Aly hit Mariah with a cordless phone. The sight of Mariah with a black eye and a swollen nose brought Mary to tears. On another day Mary caught Aly picking dirt and crud off the bottom of her sneakers and eating it. At the dinner table Aly would grab food and shove it into her mouth. When Mary would drop Aly off at daycare, she'd hear the other children say, "Oh, no, here comes Aly." That broke her heart.

"When is her mother coming to get her?" Mariah asked. "Please, Mom, send her home. She's mean."

Returning Aly to Child Services would have been the easy, maybe even the smart thing to do. Yet Mary decided to keep Aly past the original two weeks. Before long, the caseworkers began pressuring Mary to adopt Aly; they couldn't find a family willing to take her. But what about Mariah? Could Mary help Aly without hurting her own daughter? It didn't seem possible. For weeks Mary agonized over the decision.

Finally a caseworker told Mary she had to make up her mind. "We need to find a home for Aly immediately," she said.

"I need more time," Mary told her.

"We don't have more time. We need to place her now."

"Fine, do what you have to do," Mary said, holding back tears. "Send another family out."

The next day, a couple in their forties came to Mary's house to spend the day with Aly. Mary knew that giving this family the chance to adopt Aly meant she might be losing that chance herself. Ever since Aly had called her Mom, Mary felt herself drawn to the child. More than that, she felt responsible for the girl's welfare. But she had to think about Mariah.

Mary watched the couple put Aly in their car and drive away. Then she went to her bedroom, drew the curtains closed, lay on her bed, and cried.

A few hours later, Mary heard the car pull up. She watched from her porch as the woman stepped out of the car carrying Aly. Aly was thrashing and flailing and trying to lunge out of the woman's arms. Mary realized what was happening: Aly was fighting to get back to her.

Mary walked down the porch steps, and Aly threw herself into her arms. In that instant, a clear and powerful thought formed in Mary's mind: *This child belongs to me.*

"We had a very nice time," the woman said. "We went to a pool and we all went swimming. Aly had fun."

But Mary was hardly listening. She knew what she needed to do. Aly gripped her legs. But knowing didn't make the decision any easier.

"Mom, why do we want to keep Aly?" Mariah asked. "You, me, and Dad make a great triangle."

"Yes," Mary responded, "but we could be a really great diamond."

Mary had never felt so sure—and at the same time so unsure—about a decision in her life. That is when she called me.

––––

"The Other Side cannot advise you about Aly," I told Mary in our reading, "because the decision is part of your soul test. It is yours to make. This is about you discovering your true path and purpose in life. What happens next will be decided by you."

I knew this wasn't what Mary wanted to hear; I knew she was hoping for specific guidance.

During the reading, and before Mary told me, the Other Side had shown me that there was another family willing to take Aly. "They have no children of their own, and they are available to adopt her," I told Mary. "There is already a connection there. I'm seeing that you gave this other family a chance. You made the decision to let Aly go and it was painful, because that is one of the possibilities on the thread of possibilities. Aly could wind up somewhere else. There are many doorways for Aly, and some of them are not good paths."

There were no answers for Mary, but the Other Side was trying to comfort her, because of her anguish.

"You must understand that no matter what happens, you have already given Aly so much," I said. "You have already had a great impact on her life."

"But what about Mariah?" Mary asked.

I listened hard, and the words tumbled out of my mouth.

"Going forward," I said, "you must let love guide you. There will only be one signpost going forward, and that is love. When you make your decision, let love be your guide, not fear. Always let love guide you."

———

Today, nearly ten years after that reading, life in Mary's Pennsylvania home is more chaotic than ever.

Since 2005 she has adopted five special-needs children. One was born addicted to drugs. Another was adopted but was sent back by her adoptive parents. Another had been viciously abused. All of them had spent years in the system, bouncing from one foster home to another, until they met Mary.

When Mary talks about them, it is with love and admiration for how far they've come. When she first met them "they were the worst of the worst," she said. "If they weren't here they'd probably be in hospitals or prisons or psychiatric wards or dead. They make Aly look like she never had a problem. But I love them so much and I'm home-schooling them and we are like our own special little classroom. Our own little utopia. The youngest one got angry about something and yelled, 'I want to leave here,' and I said, 'You don't get to leave here, you are part of this family. We have a forever relationship.'"

Mary isn't raising the children all on her own. She has her wonderful husband, of course, and she has Mariah, who has grown into a beautiful, sensitive, giving young woman who adores and helps nurture her adopted sisters.

And Mary has one other very special helper around the house. She has her daughter, Aly.

Back in 2005, after our reading, Mary decided to adopt Aly.

"It was one of the hardest decisions of my life, but also one of the best," she says. "Aly has become the most loving person. She struggles with articulation and with other things, but she's been able to absorb what I needed her to absorb in order for her to feel safe in her life. When I got her she couldn't read or even talk. Now she reads 130 words a minute and she can express what she's feeling. She will make a heart with her hands and say, 'I love you, Mom.' She is a great hugger. She is one of the most loving people I've ever known."

In one of Aly's evaluation folders, a caseworker had written, "I doubt there is any help for her. She is too damaged." But Mary saw something no one else did. "I saw Aly's lightness of spirit," she says. "She just needed to be taught how to love." Mary and Aly underwent attachment therapy to re-create all the important bonding moments that had been missing from Aly's life.

"One day Aly came up to me and said, 'Mommy, I came out of your belly, right?'" Mary remembers. "And I said, 'What do you think?' And Aly said, 'I think I came out of your belly.' And I said, 'Okay.'"

Together, Mary and Aly created their own history as mother and daughter, and it began with Mary's understanding that her path in life was not necessarily the easy path. "I knew I wanted to keep Aly and that I was meant to keep her, but I didn't want to keep her if that meant hurting Mariah," Mary says. But keeping Aly turned out to be a great blessing for Mariah, too.

"My whole life changed because of Aly and my sisters," Mariah now says. "I have learned so much from them. I see how much they love me, and how pure and unconditional and limitless their love is. And that makes me want to be the person my sisters think I am. It makes me want to live up to their love." In fact, Mariah is planning to study occupational therapy so she can help children like Aly.

Looking back, Mary Steffey realizes that powerful forces were at work when she made her decision to become Aly's mother. Love was the key to her decision. "What helped me understand it all was love," she says. "Not just my love for Aly, but Aly's love for me. And Aly's love for Mariah. Ever since I made that decision, my life has been infinitely more blessed."

16

Forever Family

IN MY SECOND YEAR as a teacher I took a job at a Long Island high school that had about fourteen hundred students and was consistently ranked among the best public high schools in the state. It had sixteen sports teams, two dozen Advanced Placement courses, and thriving music and theater clubs. I loved it there and felt instantly at home.

As a result, my confidence as a teacher took off. The same thing was happening with my abilities—the more I worked on them, the better I got. The progress I was making on both fronts was thrilling. I realized these two parallel paths weren't as separate as I'd thought.

Being a psychic medium helped me to grow as a teacher. My gift helped me understand the importance of honoring the connections between the students and me. It gave me insight into who the students were and what they needed.

In the same way, my experiences as a teacher helped me clarify and refine my abilities. They helped me realize my readings were about learning, questioning, exploring—and not so much about answers. In both capacities I had the same goal: to help people reach their true potential.

Even so, I was careful to keep these two aspects of my life separate. It's not that I was ashamed of my work as a psychic medium; I just didn't want to risk losing my teaching job. I couldn't be certain how people would react, and I worried that if my students knew about it, it might become a distraction. So I made sure no one at school knew about my other identity—not the students, not the other teachers, and certainly not the principal.

There were times when during a routine conversation with a colleague information would come through for that person. If I felt it needed to be shared, I'd be careful to say something like, "Here's what I think . . ." or "I've got a feeling . . ." But once while I was talking with Jon, a teacher I was friendly with and whose energy I liked, a flood of information came through. Before I knew it, I found myself sharing it with him.

"You know, Jon, your car is about to break down," I told him. "Also, you and your girlfriend are going to break up. But don't worry, both of these things will lead to something better. A better car, and soon you'll meet a new girl, too, and the next girl is the one you're going to marry."

Jon looked at me strangely.

"Are you . . . ?" he said after a baffled pause.

"Don't tell anyone," I said, "but yes."

Fortunately, Jon kept my secret safe. Plus, the information I gave him proved true. He and his then girlfriend broke up, but he met a new girl right after, and ended up marrying her. And his car did break down, but he started driving a much better car. I think the Other Side really wanted to give him a heads-up so that instead of feeling deflated when these seemingly bad things happened, he would understand that it was all part of a bigger plan.

My private readings were going well, but I felt the urge to expand on what I was doing. I was driven to help as many people as I could to see a clearer path in their lives. I wanted them to know they weren't alone. I also felt compelled to help people who were grieving. I wanted to help them navigate their grief and feel the presence of their loved ones in their lives.

I'd heard about an organization called the Forever Family Foundation (FFF), whose mission was to "establish the continuity of the family, even though a member has left the physical world." They were very science-based and devoted to fostering research into the afterlife. All the work they did was not-for-profit, and the psychic mediums accredited by the FFF were all volunteers.

The organization was conceived and brought to life by Bob and Phran Ginsberg. Bob is warm and soft-spoken, with kind eyes and a mischievous smile. Phran is a pretty brunette with remarkable inner strength. Phran was deeply intuitive and occasionally had otherworldly experiences—she might see a man working on his car, for instance, and know immediately what he needed to fix, and once she told Bob she was going to win a new car, and two days later, at a Tupperware Rally, she won a green Ford Pinto. Still, she never gave too much credence to those abilities.

On a September night in 2002, Phran awoke from an intense dream, frightened. She later told Bob she feared something terrible was going to happen that day. "Let's be careful out there," she said.

That night the Ginsbergs went out to dinner at a Chinese restaurant on Long Island with their eldest son, Jon, and their pretty, buoyant youngest daughter, Bailey, fifteen. After the meal Phran and Bob went home in their car while Jon and Bailey got into his Mazda Miata. Phran and Bob made a detour to pick up some milk. On their way home they came upon an accident.

On a narrow curving two-lane road, with water on one side and a grassy knoll on the other, an SUV coming from the opposite direction had hit the Miata. The only damage to the SUV was a broken headlight, but the Miata had been totally demolished on the passenger side, where Bailey had been sitting.

Jon was airlifted to a hospital a few miles east. Bob went with him. Bailey was rushed by ambulance to Huntington Hospital. Phran was driven in a police car behind the ambulance. Along the way paramedics resuscitated Bailey several times.

At the hospital, Phran, terrified and in shock, sat in the waiting room while doctors worked on Bailey. For a few moments she drifted to sleep, and in those moments she had a vivid dream. In the dream, she saw herself sitting in the passenger seat of the Miata. She saw the SUV coming from the other direction in the wrong lane, directly at her. She saw Jon pull the wheel hard left to avoid the collision, exposing the passenger side. And she saw the SUV ram the Miata, sending it end over end.

The crash in the dream startled Phran awake. She called her husband and said, "I know how it happened."

Soon a doctor came out to see Phran. The damage to Bailey's organs was devastating, and there was no more they could do. "Bailey died in the hospital just a few hours after the crash," says Phran. "It was the worst day of my life."

Bailey's brother survived the crash but didn't remember it at all. Inexplicably, the police at the scene let the other driver go without questioning her, and she disappeared without a trace. There was no way for Bob and Phran to know what had happened, except for Phran's dream.

A few weeks later, Bob asked his wife, "How did you know how the crash happened?"

"I don't know," Phran said. "I just knew."

The answer made Bob angry.

"He was thinking, if I knew, if there was some unseen force

that told me what had happened, then why wasn't I able to stop it *before* it happened?" says Phran. "He was mad at me. He didn't understand. It was his way of dealing with the grief."

A few months later, an insurance company hired an accident reconstruction expert to re-create the crash. The expert's report confirmed Phran's rendition of the accident. But that only raised more questions. How had Phran known? Why had she dreamed it? Who had given her the information?

"We needed answers," says Bob. "We felt like there was something happening we should know about."

Bob and Phran got the idea that maybe, in that mysterious space where life and dreams intersect, some measure of solace might be found for grieving parents like them. Maybe the whole story of their daughter's life and death—so far an unacceptably simple story in which beautiful Bailey was here one day and gone the next—had yet to be told.

So they read books about psychic phenomena. They went to see mediums. They opened their minds to a new way of looking at everything. All that digging led to one inescapable conclusion. "There is an unseen world," Bob says, "and we were meant to work with it."

Bob and Phran teamed up with Dr. Gary E. Schwartz—a professor of psychology, medicine, neurology, psychiatry, and surgery, and the director of the Laboratory for Advances in Consciousness and Health at the University of Arizona—and cofounded the Forever Family Foundation. Through it they would help grieving people by trying to connect them with the loved ones they had lost, building a bridge between this world and the next. It would be Bailey's bridge.

———

In 2005 I contacted the FFF and said I was a psychic medium interested in volunteering my services. The first requirement, I was told, was to pass a rigorous certification test. It involved doing several readings in quick succession, while being scored for accuracy.

On a hot August day I found myself, along with four other mediums, in a conference room in a hotel on Long Island. A couple of the other mediums seemed to know each other, which made me feel like the new kid on the first day of school. I wasn't friends with any psychic mediums, and I wasn't part of any psychic medium community. There were very few people I could talk to about my gift.

We were led into a large ballroom where the tests were held. A middle-aged man was brought in and seated in front of all the mediums. We were asked to read him silently for fifteen minutes and write down what came through on a legal pad.

I was nervous. I'd never been asked to read in public, and I certainly had never had my readings scored. I focused hard on the man and scribbled down everything that came through.

When the fifteen minutes were up, an FFF staffer told us the man's name was Tom. The woman sitting next to me elbowed me excitedly.

"Check this out!" she said, pointing to her legal pad. On it she had written *Tom*.

I smiled politely. All I'd gotten was that his name began with *T*. Still, something in that brief exchange with the woman— I learned she was a psychic medium named Kim Russo—calmed me down. It felt like we were there in the trenches together, maybe even peers. That strange feeling of camaraderie was oddly comforting.

Next we were moved to one of five stations set up in separate alcoves, each with a video camera capturing the results. At each station there was a sitter holding a clipboard. The sitter was not allowed to talk to us; he or she could only say yes or no. Once the readings began, the mediums would be given fifteen minutes to read each sitter before being rotated to the next station for another fifteen-minute reading. The sitters would score our readings for accuracy. That part of the test, through all five stations, would take seventy-five minutes.

Nervously I sat down at my first station and took a deep breath. Then I looked at the woman across from me, the sitter. I swam into the space between us and linked my energy with hers and with the Other Side. The nervousness went away. I stopped thinking about who I was or what I was doing, I just listened to the Other Side and shared what those there were saying.

The woman's father came through, and then her aunt and maternal grandmother. They gave me dates that were important to her family. They showed me how family members had crossed. They brought up the work she was currently having done on her house. The Other Side poured out information, and before I knew it, it was time to move to the next sitter.

By the third sitter, I felt completely open to the Other Side. I was reading for a woman who appeared to be in her forties. Her son came through immediately. He gave me his name and told me he had passed in a car accident. Then he did something strange—he showed me the date of my daughter Ashley's birthday, which is May 16.

"Did your son cross on May 16?" I asked the sitter.

Her face went pale and her lip trembled. Her eyes filled with tears.

"Yes," she said.

Her son started making jokes from the Other Side. He brought up funny family stories. Through her tears, the woman laughed, and so did I. I didn't want to leave her when our time was up.

The next sitter—a woman in her early thirties—had also lost a son. He told me his name was Michael and that he had passed from cancer. He showed me three years on a timeline, which meant he'd crossed three years ago. And he, too, made his mother laugh, by talking about his pickiness with food. Then he thanked her for the love she had shown him while he was here.

"That was his lesson," I explained. "To feel your unconditional love. That was why he was here. And he completed that lesson. He says to tell you he always felt safe, even when he was crossing. He crossed surrounded by your love."

I read for one more person, and then the test was complete—the video cameras were turned off, the clipboards put down. I was exhausted. I felt that I had done well in the readings, and I realized I'd learned something new. I was amazed by the son who informed me of his crossing date by showing me Ashley's birthday. Somehow he'd been able to use my own frame of reference in order to pass on the message. I realized that the Other Side has access to every thought, every moment, every intimate detail of my life—and that those there will use that access to pass along messages and validations to their loved ones.

Phran told us we would hear from the FFF in a few weeks with the results. We learned the sitters in front of us were professional sitters—people who'd been trained not to reveal anything during readings, to root out tricks and gimmicks and fraudulent readings.

I milled around the conference room and found myself next to Kim Russo and another psychic medium, Bobbi Allison. Kim and Bobbi were already friends. They were both around my age, pretty, smart, and completely down to earth. I loved their energy. We chatted about the test and compared notes, letting go of our nervousness. Our conversation was casual; it felt like three friends talking.

"Who's your teacher?" Bobbi asked me.

"My teacher?" I said. "I don't have a teacher."

Kim and Bobbi looked shocked. I didn't realize until that moment that not having a teacher or mentor was unusual. They told me about their mentors and how they'd helped guide them to explore their gifts further. They spoke of their teachers with great love and admiration, as if they couldn't have become who they were without them.

We made plans to get together, and a couple of weeks later met for dinner at a restaurant near where we lived. We picked up right where we left off. Each of us told the story of when we first realized we were different. Kim explained how she'd close her eyes to go to sleep and receive visions of people she didn't know. "I was seeing dead people in my bedroom when I was nine," she said.

Bobbi told us how her grandmother, mother, and three sisters were all psychic. "I was always reading people," she said. "People began to call me Miss Know-It-All. Even my family got fed up. They'd tell me they were going to leave me at home when they went out because I always spoiled things with all my 'knowing.'"

My dinner with Kim and Bobbi was exhilarating. I felt a lightness of spirit that I hadn't felt in a long time, if ever. We bounced ideas off each other, compared techniques, and even read for each other. It was just like any three girlfriends giving each other advice, only the advice was coming from the Other Side.

This bonding was meaningful for each of us. "It's hard to keep yourself balanced with all the readings," Bobbi said at one point. "You have to find your balance. And being with friends who have the same energy is how I stay balanced."

I knew what she was talking about. We all had the same fears and problems. We all needed a safe place just to be ourselves. Before that night, I'd felt like I was out there by myself. Now, though, I had a kind of psychic family. We would go on to meet for dinner once a month to talk, laugh, sympathize, and support. I had a sisterhood now. I had a safe place.

—

A few weeks after the certification test, I got a call from Phran Ginsberg. She explained how my test had been graded—how each sitter provided numerical scores that were used to calculate my accuracy. Phran said my scores were high, meaning that my readings had been exceptionally accurate.

"Congratulations," she said. "You are now certified."

I felt my heart race and my eyes well up. I was approved to participate in FFF-sponsored events. I'd found the outlet I needed to take my abilities to the next level. I felt the pull to help people who were grieving, and now I'd get the chance to do it. Being certified by the FFF was a powerful validation for me—but it was more than that. It was also a galvanizing moment. It was a call to action. I was now part of something greater than myself.

I was part of a team of light.

I had the feeling my life as a psychic medium was about to change.

17

More Things in
Heaven and Earth

ASHLEY HAD JUST TURNED FIVE when Garrett and I
decided it was the right time to have another baby.

We had always wanted another child but felt we needed to wait
a bit. Our lives were hectic, often chaotic, with Garrett finishing
law school and then studying for the bar exam, and with me as a
new mom, a new teacher, and a psychic medium on the side. In
time things began to settle down. Garrett passed the bar, and I
received tenure as a teacher. We were able to scrimp and save and
buy a one-story, three-bedroom home on a quiet, tree-lined street
on Long Island. I told the universe I was ready. It was baby time.

But when I didn't get pregnant immediately, I began to question the universe. Was this meant to happen now or not? To help
things along I went to my local pharmacy to buy an over-the-
counter ovulation predictor. I took Ashley with me.

I found myself in an aisle surrounded by two walls of pregnancy tests, ovulation predictors, and all sorts of baby-making

products. I felt overwhelmed. I started thinking that I might not get pregnant, and felt bereft. I was giving in to my fears. I did my best to hide my feelings from Ashley, but inside I was a wreck.

Just then, Ashley tugged on my shirt.

"Mommy," she said, "do you know Fuzzle is lying right by your feet now, giving you love?"

Fuzzle?

Fuzzle had been our family dog when I was a little girl. She was a beautiful, affectionate West Highland White Terrier, and I loved her like crazy. Fuzzle always comforted me and gave me love when I needed it. She was loyal beyond belief. When we went on family vacations Fuzzle would snuggle on top of one of our suitcases the night before, so we wouldn't forget to take her. I adored Fuzzle like any girl adores her first pet, and I vowed to keep her with me in my heart forever. But even so, it's not like I thought about Fuzzle all the time. After all, she'd crossed nearly two decades before. I was sure I'd mentioned her to Ashley, and she may have even seen a photo of her, but honestly, Fuzzle didn't come up all that often in our daily lives.

And now my five-year-old daughter was telling me Fuzzle was curled up at my feet in the pregnancy aisle of the drugstore?

Immediately, I knew it was true.

I'd already had suspicions that Ashley possessed some of the same gifts as I did, so I wasn't all that surprised she could see Fuzzle. But I was overcome with emotion that Fuzzle would show up with a message of love just when I needed it. All my doubts and fears about getting pregnant vanished in that moment. I had the strong sensation that everything would be fine.

One month later, I was pregnant.

———

Being pregnant again filled me with joy and energy. Nine months later a beautiful baby boy arrived in the world with a crown of shining platinum-blond hair. He seemed to glow. We named him Hayden.

I expected the months after his birth to be busy and draining and difficult, but also happy and glorious, just as they had been after Ashley was born. But this time it was different. Instead of feeling elated, I felt depressed, anxious, and pulled down by negative energy. It wasn't Hayden's fault; he was a sweet, buoyant little baby. It was just something the pregnancy did to my internal wiring. I felt swings of energy and emotion—like living in a house where the thermostat went from hot to cold to hot. At times it felt like a cloud of darkness was hovering over me.

Was it postpartum depression? My symptoms certainly matched the diagnosis—sadness, anxiety, irritability, crying episodes, disrupted sleep. But I also had another frightening symptom: I began to have dark thoughts.

It wasn't that I'd ever do something bad and harmful—God knows I never would. It was that I realized I could. And no matter how hard I tried to will positive thoughts to blot out the negative ones, I couldn't overcome them. The dark thoughts just wouldn't stop. It was terrifying. *This isn't me,* I told myself over and over. *I work in the light, not the dark. I don't even watch scary movies!* A familiar feeling came roaring back: *What if I'm crazy?*

I had to face the reality that something might seriously be wrong with me, just as I'd suspected for most of my life. All the progress I'd made toward accepting my abilities, toward finding my place in the world, was suddenly at risk. It was a painful, agonizing time.

I decided to seek help, and made an appointment to see a psychiatrist.

———

When I walked into Dr. Marc Reitman's office I was a bundle of raw nerves. Would talk about the Other Side make me appear psychotic? Might Dr. Reitman find me unfit to take care of my children?

His manner quickly put me at ease. His energy was soft and gentle and loving. Still, I feared the worst.

I began by telling him about my terrifying thoughts. I held nothing back. Dr. Reitman listened quietly, betraying no emotion or judgment. When I was done, he asked me a simple question.

"I know you have these dark thoughts, but do you think you would ever actually act on them?" he asked.

I didn't hesitate. "Absolutely not," I said. "Not in a million years. I would never, ever do anything like that."

"Okay, then," Dr. Reitman said.

I felt relieved, but I knew I had to tell him the rest.

"That's not all," I said. I told him about how I knew my grandfather was going to die when I was eleven. About the dream I had about John. About how I felt people's energy and saw them in colors. About how I talk to the dead, and how they respond. About how they have me pass along messages to their loved ones.

Dr. Reitman listened stoically. I dreaded his answer.

"Let me ask you something, Laura," he asked calmly. "When you do these readings, do you get accurate information? Does it help people?"

"Oh, yes," I told him, "I get names and dates and all sorts of validating details. And the messages are always about healing and love. The readings are beautiful. I learn so much from them myself. I love being part of them."

Dr. Reitman smiled and looked me in the eye.

"I don't think you're crazy," he said. "You should not think of these things as symptoms of anything. You should see them as skills you need to explore. The universe is bigger than we know."

In those few words, those magical, healing words, I heard the beautiful echo of my beloved William Shakespeare, who through Hamlet said, "There are more things in heaven and earth, Horatio, than are dreamt of in your philosophy."

I felt free. My biggest fear—that I was crazy, delusional—was lifted. It felt like I had passed some kind of psychological test.

Dr. Reitman addressed the symptoms of my postpartum depression. He devised a treatment plan that began with putting me on medication to help me deal with the mood swings and dark thoughts. The problem was, I don't metabolize medicine in the way most people do. I have an extremely low tolerance for any kind of drug. Even a tablet of ibuprofen can make me feel weak and out of whack. But we agreed to try it.

Within a few weeks, I found the medicine wasn't helping me with the mood swings. It was also interfering with my abilities. Instead of the fast flow of information I normally got during a reading, what I was getting now was more of a steady drip. Dr. Reitman decided to try me on a natural mood balancer called SAM-e.

That did the trick. The dark thoughts evaporated, like a heavy fog being burned off by the sun. The natural flow of information from the Other Side returned. In fact, it intensified, just as it had after Ashley's birth.

I stayed on SAM-e for a number of months until I felt fully balanced. But just as important as Dr. Reitman's treatment of my postpartum symptoms was his acceptance of my gift. There was nothing in his training as a psychiatrist that touched on the supernatural, but it was my good fortune that he was open to things not found in psychiatric texts.

I went to see Dr. Reitman several times in the months that followed. I felt safe and free to discuss my abilities with him, and the more we talked, the less unsure and isolated I felt.

Was I just lucky to find a psychiatrist with such a curious, nonjudgmental mind? I don't think it was luck. The Other Side, it seemed, was always putting special people in my path—people who were meant to help me understand and honor my abilities. Dr. Reitman was one of them.

18

The Policeman's Cap

WITH MY ENERGY and my abilities rebalanced, I was ready to do readings again. Around that time I got a call from Phran Ginsberg at the Forever Family Foundation, inviting me to participate in a special event called "How to Listen When Your Children Speak." Ten sets of parents who had lost a child would be there, along with one psychic medium: me.

I swallowed hard and told Phran I'd do it.

The event was scheduled for the last week in August. In the weeks leading up to it, I felt my anxiety escalating. It was like an internal buzzing that got louder and louder until it was nearly unbearable. I spent a lot of time talking to the Other Side, asking them to please be there and give me messages for these grieving families. This event was unlike anything I'd experienced. I'd have to walk into a room with nothing but my inner screen. No plan B, no other medium to pick up the slack should the Other Side fail to come through for me. I would have to trust the Other Side completely.

I spent the week before the event with my children, enjoying the last days of summer. Hayden, who was sixteen months, and Ashley, then seven, kept me busy and took my mind off the event. Still, when the day of the event arrived, I was more nervous than ever. The buzzing was at a fever pitch. I tried to eat, but I could barely keep food down. I skipped dinner altogether.

Garrett was working as an in-house attorney for a large retail chain, and he wasn't due home until six-thirty. My mom came over to babysit until he got home. I kissed the kids, thanked my mom, and climbed into my Honda Pilot. I called Garrett from the car, and once again he assured me I'd be fine. When we hung up I focused on my breathing. *Breathe in, breathe out. Find your center. Connect with your spiritual self.*

And then, on Jericho Turnpike, the children came.

I pulled off the road and screeched into the Staples parking lot. I took out a little notebook I keep in my purse and wrote down as much as I could of what the children were saying. Even as it was happening, I could hardly believe it. I'd never been so barraged by messages from the Other Side before.

After a few minutes I got back on Jericho Turnpike and raced to the Huntington Hilton. I got to the event just in time. The parents were already seated in the conference room, yet it was eerily quiet. It seemed airless. I could feel the heaviness all around me.

"This is Laura Lynne Jackson," Bob Ginsberg told the parents. "She's a Certified Medium with the Forever Family Foundation, and she's here tonight to help us learn how to talk to our children."

Bob and Phran slipped out of the room to give the parents as much privacy as possible. As soon as they left, everyone's attention turned back to me. As a teacher, I was used to people staring at me and waiting for me to talk, but this was different. The silence was excruciating. I had to do something—I had to start talking. But I didn't know what to say.

Then I realized that all I needed to do was let the children talk. And all at once, I felt them rush in.

"Your children are here," I blurted out. "And there is something they want you to know."

Without even noticing it, I had slipped into that place that is just slightly above the level of my head—the place where I cease to inhabit my physical body and become my spiritual self, where I am no longer the "me" I know, and where I can let go of my earthly concerns. I felt a click and a door opening.

The children appeared as points of light on my inner screen. They came through clearly and strongly, and it was exhilarating. I was surrounded by these beautiful kids with all their beautiful energy.

"Your children are all here together, around you now," I told the parents. "And collectively they have a message they want you to hear. They are saying, 'Please don't worry about us. We are fine. We are okay. Put your fears and worries aside, so we can have this time together. There is so much we want you to know.'"

I sensed that these words cut right through the tension in the room. Some of the heaviness lifted. I understood why the children had come to me before the event, in my car. They knew their parents would have their guard up. They knew their parents had built walls around themselves to block out the pain and grief and rage. The children knew those walls could keep them from being heard. So they came to me with a common message for all the parents: *Take down the walls, let down your guard, so we can come through. Don't be afraid or confused or resistant. Please know we are here with you, beside you, right now.*

These children, so vibrant and so full of light, were inviting us to swim in their happy energy. I felt nothing but pure love. No fear, no pain, no guilt—just love. It's like when you're waiting at the airport for someone you dearly love, and all of a sudden that person turns a corner and you see him or her walking toward you, and it's just the best feeling in the world. That's how I felt in that conference room. I felt embraced by love.

This time, to my surprise, the children lined up patiently, one by one, instead of overwhelming me as they had in the car. I wasn't dictating the order of events, they were. I sensed a child coming through and felt a strong pull—I call it an energy lasso, the feeling of the Other Side guiding my body—toward a couple at the far end of the conference table. The man was stoic, refusing to let any emotion play on his face. His wife sat close to him but did not touch him. She was already crying.

The child coming through was a teenage girl. She showed me she was an only child, in order to acknowledge the particular grief her parents felt when she passed. She showed me the letter *J*, but she also showed me a short word, as if to say she went by a nickname.

"Your child is coming through," I said to her parents. "Your daughter. She is showing me a *J* name, but she went by something else. Jessica or Jennifer, but you called her something else."

Her parents nodded slowly. Her name was Jessica, but they called her Jessie.

Then Jessie showed me what happened to her.

"It started in her chest," I said.

Later, I would learn the whole story from her parents. On the morning of Good Friday, 2007, Jessie, a high school sophomore, came down the stairs of her family's home in Falls River, Connecticut. She told her parents, "I feel sick."

"Jessie, there's no school today," her father, Joe, said. "You don't have to pretend to be sick."

"No, I really am," she said. "I really don't feel well."

Just the day before, Jessie had played in a lacrosse game and gone to a training session with the state police's Explorer Club for teens, two of her many passions. Smart and pretty, with red hair, freckles, and a warm, shy smile, Jessie never slowed down—by fifteen she was already an honor student, a second-degree black belt, and a certified scuba diver. She loved her friends, her family, and her golden retriever, Paladin (Pal for short), and she had a great curiosity about life.

She was turning sixteen in two weeks, and she'd just started seeing her first boyfriend.

"Nothing serious," her mother, Maryann, said. "She just told me, 'Mom, I love someone,' like teenagers do."

Joe and Maryann drove Jessie to her pediatrician, who said she had the flu. That night Jessie coughed up blood, and her parents took her to a hospital. The next day an ambulance rushed her to another medical center, and from there Jessie was airlifted to the Children's Hospital in Boston. She did have the flu, but it was a rare and virulent strain.

Quickly the flu turned into pneumonia, then sepsis. Jessie's vital signs were weakening, and she was put on a respirator because her lungs were so damaged. Friends and relatives drove to Boston to be with Joe and Maryann, while others stayed behind and held a candlelight vigil in Jessie's backyard.

Then, just five days after she came down the stairs on Good Friday, a CAT scan revealed Jessie had bleeding in her brain. The doctors said there was nothing they could do.

Joe, a burly man who works in an auto body shop, and Maryann, a strong Catholic woman, went numb. Something they didn't even have time to anticipate was suddenly, unimaginably coming to pass. They were losing their beautiful girl.

Joe and Maryann went into Jessie's room together to say goodbye.

"I love you," Maryann told her, stroking her daughter's long red hair. "You are our best friend in the world."

Joe held tight to Jessie's hand and rubbed the tears out of his eyes so they wouldn't fall on her. "I love you, Jessie," he said. "I love you so much."

Jessie passed away a few days after Easter.

Joe and Maryann left Jessie's bedroom just the way it was, as if they expected her to come bouncing in any minute. To stay busy, they focused on the memorial service and funeral. Instead of birthday gifts, they picked out a headstone.

"Nothing made sense," says Joe. "It made zero sense. Jessie was here, and then she wasn't here. Why did this happen? Why Jessie? Why are we even here, any of us, if something like this can just happen?"

"We questioned our faith in life," says Maryann. "We were searching and grasping for answers, but there were none. Life didn't have any purpose, not with Jessie gone. Why do we get to be here, and not her?"

I didn't know the extent of their despair as I stood before them in the conference room. But I knew Jessie hadn't just disappeared. She was right there with us, full of love and life. And she had a million things to say.

"She wants to thank you for the butterflies," I told Joe and Maryann.

They looked at each other, and Maryann reached for a tissue. I didn't know why butterflies were meaningful, and I didn't have to. Clearly her parents did. I later learned that Joe and Maryann had recently chosen their daughter's gravestone, and they picked a stone carved with butterflies floating above Jessie's name. Jessie had loved butterflies.

But that was just the beginning.

"She is showing me an animal," I went on. "A cat. A cat in a tree. A cat stuck on a branch in a tree?" I looked at Joe and Maryann for affirmation, but there was none. That was okay—I knew that sometimes messages from the Other Side don't make sense until later. I asked them to remember her message, since it might be validated at a later time. (A few weeks after the reading, Joe was raking leaves in the backyard when he saw Jessie's favorite stuffed cat wedged in a tree branch. Instantly he remembered why it was there. She'd forgotten it in the yard one day, and he'd picked it up and absently put it in the tree so the family's golden retriever wouldn't chew it up. The detail hadn't clicked with him in the conference room. But Jessie had shared it so Joe could carry this detail around with him and make sense of it just when he most needed to feel his daughter's presence.)

Jessie kept on going.

"I'm seeing a hat, sort of like a policeman's cap," I said. "Jessie is showing me a blue policeman's cap. I'm supposed to talk to you about the hat. Are you a policeman?"

Joe looked startled. More than that—stunned. Later, he explained the significance of the policeman's cap.

Before she died, Jessie had gone to a camp for teens run by the state police department. It was just the kind of thing that Jessie, an adventurous soul, loved doing. Joe gave her $50 and asked her to buy him a policeman's cap. But Jessie spent the money on something else and forgot to buy the cap. No one thought anything of it.

Then, at Jessie's funeral, something inexplicable happened. A police officer came up to Joe. The two men had never met. In the officer's hand was a blue policeman's cap.

The policeman struggled to find the right words.

"I got this hat for you," he told Joe, his eyes filling with tears. "I don't know why, I really don't. I just know I'm supposed to give it to you."

Joe took the hat in his hand, turned it around and around, and stared at it. Then he hugged the cop.

The Other Side, it seems, can make just about anyone a messenger, as long as the person chosen is willing to keep his or her heart and mind open to the Other Side. The policeman could have ignored his strange compulsion to give Joe a cap. Luckily, he didn't.

Jessie showed me the hat because it was something only Joe and Maryann would know about. Not even the police officer knew why the cap was significant. But Jessie wanted me to share it so her parents would know that she was there with them in the conference room.

Next she showed me her illness. She showed me her whole body, which I understood meant that she had had an illness that affected her everywhere. Then she brought me up to her head. She was showing me her illness had spread and affected her brain. She also showed me a three-day timeline—it was a fast-moving illness.

"It poisoned her whole system," I told her parents. "It went through her blood and up into her brain. When it moved into her brain is when you had to let her go."

Joe and Maryann had never told anyone—anyone—about the bleeding in Jessie's brain. They never told anyone that it was the reason they'd taken her off life support. But Jessie showed it to me, to offer further proof that she was there. Maybe she knew her parents needed a lot of convincing. Maybe she knew that of all the details, that would be the one that truly convinced them she was present. And it was.

"This is what Jessie wants to tell you," I said. "She wants you to understand she has not left you. She is never going to leave you. She is always going to be your daughter, and she will always love you. You haven't lost her and you will never lose her. Please understand you can never lose her."

In the hospital, on the day Jessie died, Maryann had held her hand, stroked her hair, and said, "You are our best friend in the world." And now, three months later, in a conference room on Long Island, Jessie took those beautiful words and brought them right back to her parents.

"Jessie isn't gone," I said. "Jessie will never be gone. She is with you always. And she will always be your best friend."

19

The Final Child

THAT NIGHT IN THE CONFERENCE ROOM, the children kept coming: boys and girls, some as young as five, some in their teens, some even older. They gave me clear identifying details to prove to their parents they were there, before having me stress, over and over, how much they needed their parents to know they weren't truly gone.

I was pulled toward a man and woman whose daughter had been killed while riding her bike. She wanted to tell them to let go of their guilt—that there was nothing they could have done to prevent what happened.

"And she wants to thank you for putting her artwork up in the living room," I said, "so that she could still be present in your lives."

One young man came through and showed me he had drowned along with two of his friends. "He wants you to know that he crossed with his friends, that he was never alone," I told his parents. "And when he got to the Other Side his grandfather and the family dog were waiting there to greet him."

All the children who came through wanted the same thing—to somehow ease their loved ones' pain and anguish. They made it so their parents could see a glimmer of light from the Other Side, and just that tiny glimmer allowed them to see a pathway out of their darkness.

The readings went on and on. I didn't realize it, but more than three hours had passed since I'd started. So much had happened in those three hours, and a powerful sense of relief, of hope, filled the once morbid room. The people who were going home that night were not the same people who had arrived. Their torment had been lessened—not ended, but lessened. Their children had given them the most beautiful, magical, powerful gift—the understanding that they weren't gone.

I was exhausted and exhilarated and overwhelmed by all the love passed back and forth that night. But still, something wasn't right. Something felt wrong.

All of the children had come through—except for one.

I scanned the room and found a person I hadn't yet spoken to—a woman in her early forties with black hair. She was a single mother, I would later learn, and the only parent there without a spouse. She sat patiently at the very head of the conference table, but no one had come through for her. What was going on? Most of the parents had left the room when the black-haired woman slowly rose to her feet, turned, and shuffled toward the exit. I could feel her staggering disappointment. But what was I supposed to do?

And then it hit me: her child wanted to be last.

I hurried toward the woman and put my hand on her shoulder.

"Wait," I said, "please stay. I will stay late with you."

We sat at the conference table, just the two of us. And just as we settled in, someone came through for her.

This point of light was not in the upper right of my screen, the strong and clear part—it was somewhere lower. It felt like I was listening to a really low and deep vibration, something I had to concentrate on to make sense of. Plus, this person's light was much less intense than the others had been, and I had to pull my own energy down low—much lower than where it had been all evening—in order to pull hers out. That's why we had to wait for the room to empty out, I realized. This reading was different.

Finally, I could see it was a girl—a young woman, really, twenty years old. The information was faint, but I could make it out.

"You're a psychiatrist," I said to her mother. The woman's face froze. Then I saw a college building, and letters—three letters. "Your daughter is telling me she went to NYU," I said. The daughter showed me where her mother lived, and a few other details, and she showed me animals, small animals—cats.

"Your daughter wants to thank you for taking care of her cats," I said. "She is really grateful to you for being so loving with them."

The cats were the detail that did it. I could feel her mom's energy open more fully to the reading and to her daughter's messages.

Then the young woman showed me how she died, though I already knew. She had killed herself.

Suicides often come through as lower lights. This woman's daughter had waited so long to come through because she didn't want the fact of her suicide to come up in front of other parents. She'd waited until her mother had more privacy.

She showed me how she'd tried to kill herself once before, when she was sixteen, and how hard her mother had tried to help her then. Then she showed me how she'd finally done it—she'd overdosed on pills—and she showed me that she had been going to do it no matter what her mother or anyone else did. This was her choice. This was her doorway. She had stopped her soul's journey on earth, and only after she crossed did she realize what a gift life is.

I told all this to the mother, who was crying. Though it had started out weak, the connection had become strong and profound. I could feel the incredible love passing between this mother and her daughter.

And for the first time that evening, tears ran down my face. It was one of the most powerful moments I'd ever experienced.

"Your daughter wants you to know that if she had understood how bad this would be for you, how painful it would be, she never would have done it," I went on. "She is so sorry that she did it."

We were at the very heart of it now. This was what the mother most needed to hear.

"Your daughter wants to thank you," I said. "She wants to thank you for trying and for understanding. But most of all she wants to thank you for what you did for her after she passed."

In the all but empty room, I delivered the message: "Your daughter wants to thank you for forgiving her."

I stayed with the girl's mother for forty minutes. When we were done, Bob and Phran hugged me and thanked me. They were very happy with how the evening had turned out. As for me, whatever exhaustion I'd felt went away after that last reading. Instead I felt completely energized. I'd been able to help all the parents connect with their children and deliver these wonderful messages of love. The realization that I could do that—that I could play a part in this miraculous process of healing—was very meaningful for me. I knew in that moment once and for all that the abilities I had feared were a curse were actually a blessing.

I got back in my car and raced home. I was on such a high, I was still buzzing. I know that might sound strange, considering I'd just spent four hours with grieving parents talking about unthinkably sad events. But the truth was, we'd all shared a miraculous moment. The children were there, with their parents, in that room! Love goes on and on!

The night hadn't been about death and darkness at all. It had been about light and life and love.

It was 11:00 p.m. I called Garrett and told him that the evening had gone great. "I told you it would," he said.

"I'll be home soon," I said.

And just as I said that, I realized I wasn't alone in the car. The children were still with me.

It was not that they had more messages to share. It was just that they, too, were still buzzing. All of my readings have a triangle effect, with three energies at play—mine, the sitter's, and the energy of those on the Other Side. We were all feeling the same thing that night. Like me, the children were giddy. Eventually they left, but I could still feel a presence in the car. It was a child, but it wasn't one of the children who came through in the conference room. This child had a message to share, too.

I pulled into the driveway and quietly made my way inside the house. I gave Garrett a big hug and kiss and tiptoed in to see my sleeping babies. I cracked open the door to Ashley's bedroom and stood over her. She was my angel, my precious angel. I bent down, gave her a kiss on the cheek, and pulled her blanket up around her shoulders. Then I crept into Hayden's room, kissed him, and tucked him in. I ran my fingers gently over his soft hair. I tried to never take a moment with my children for granted. I knew better than that. I knew how lucky I was.

In the kitchen, I got out some chips and dip and ate like I hadn't eaten in a week. Then I told Garrett I still had a little business to attend to. I went to our bedroom and closed the door.

The night of the FFF group reading I was aware that Phran and Bob had a daughter who had passed, but I didn't know anything about her or how she'd crossed.

What I did know, as I drove home from the Huntington Hilton, was that the child in the car with me was their daughter, Bailey.

I would have phoned Bob and Phran, but I was afraid it was too late to call. Instead, I wrote them an email.

All night Bob and Phran had stayed behind the scenes. They'd sat off to the side, silently cheering on the grieving parents, pulling for their children to come through. They had put aside their own pain, their own loss, and focused on helping other parents.

But now there was a message for them.

"All the children who came through want to thank you for making the event happen," I wrote. "The Other Side tells me you are healing more people than you know.

"Bailey is so proud of you," I continued. "I saw her standing behind all the other children on my screen, beaming with pride and joy. She is so beautiful."

Bailey also wanted to mark a significant date coming up. "Is it someone's birthday or anniversary right around now in your family?" I asked. "Bailey is acknowledging an important date, and letting you know she will always be a part of your lives."

The next day Phran wrote back. She thanked me warmly for the reading and told me the anniversary of Bailey's passing was three days away.

"You surely had Bailey there with you that night," Phran wrote.

Some children are not meant to be here long. Some are here for only a short while, but in that time they learn and teach profound lessons about love. And their impact on the world doesn't end when they cross. They are always around to teach us about love. Bailey was only here for fifteen years, but she continues to change our world for the better. Because of Bob and Phran's transcendent love for her, they created the Forever Family Foundation. And now the three of them—Bob, Phran, and Bailey—work together as a team of light and healing.

20

The Trapped Bee

ABOUT A YEAR AFTER the FFF event, I read for a New York City couple, Charlie and RoseAnn. I saw that they had been married a long time and that they didn't have children. But as I further opened the door to the Other Side, a point of light appeared on my screen. I could sense that the point of light was not a person at all. It was a dog.

"I am seeing a large black dog with an *S* name," I told them. Charlie and RoseAnn told me that the first dog they had together was a lovely Doberman/Lab mix named Shadow.

More points of light came through. I was dazzled by them; they were an entirely new experience for me. It wasn't just Shadow the dog coming through. It was all kinds of different animals, points of light lined up one behind the other. The lights kept coming and coming, a whole menagerie of animals, and all with the same message. It was a message of gratitude, recognition, and love.

I felt a wave of pure love sweeping back and forth between the sitters and the Other Side. It was so intense I couldn't make out all the animals that were there. All I knew was that there were a lot of them. I wondered what Charlie and RoseAnn had done to create such a powerful exchange of love and gratitude.

—

Charlie grew up in the Bronx; RoseAnn was from Brooklyn. They were both raised in families that loved—and often saved—animals. "I had a knack for rescuing parakeets," Charlie told me. "They'd escape their cages in someone's apartment and end up on our fire escape. I'd throw a towel over them and get them inside. It wasn't easy, but I wound up with five parakeets."

For RoseAnn, it was all about feral cats and stray dogs. "There was a family of cats that lived in the storage area of our building, and my mother and I brought them in," she said. "A mother and two kittens, Blackie and Gray. We fed them and loved them and nurtured them. The dogs we already had were pretty good about having cats around."

When Charlie and RoseAnn started dating in their twenties, they bonded over their love of animals. Once they were together, many more strays wound up in their path. They didn't go around looking for animals to save. The animals in need always seemed to find them.

There was Stripes, the cat who showed up on their stoop looking banged up (she'd been hit by a car and had a broken hip). There were Stars and Fang and Mommy and Heidi and Baby and Snow, feral cats they'd found in alleyways or on the street. There was a huge tabby named Reginald Van Cat and a mutt named Farfel. "We would turn a corner in Brooklyn and see two dogs chained to a fence," says RoseAnn. "What were we supposed to do, walk away?"

But it wasn't just cats and dogs. They went shopping at a mall one day and found two baby sparrows huddled in the remnants of a nest in a shopping cart. They'd just been hatched and their eyes were closed, but they were cold to the touch. Charlie and Rose-Ann took them inside and warmed them, and against all odds, the sparrows—whom they named Heckle and Jeckle—survived. Charlie and RoseAnn found them a home in a wild bird sanctuary.

Another time they were in their apartment building's garage when they heard the faint sound of chirping. They searched for an hour to find the source of the chirping and finally found a newborn sparrow tucked behind a snow tire. It couldn't fly, so they took it outside and put it under a bush so the bird's parents could find her. When they checked back an hour later the sparrow was still there, so Charlie and RoseAnn took her in, nursed her back to health, and then set her free.

Then there were the duck and ducklings trapped on the New Jersey Turnpike with cars and trucks zipping by at 70 miles per hour. "I spotted them waddling into the left lane," RoseAnn said. "One driver braked really hard, and the ducks kept going into the center lane. Then another driver braked, and then the ducks were in front of me. And so I braked, and they kept walking across the highway onto the shoulder. I looked in my rearview mirror and saw a giant tractor-trailer bearing down on me at full speed."

RoseAnn said a quick prayer. Without slowing down and at the last second, the tractor-trailer veered onto the shoulder, around RoseAnn's car, narrowly missing both her and the ducks. It swung back onto the highway and kept going, and the ducks just kept walking. "It was as if all of us had this group consciousness and we were able to miss the ducks," says RoseAnn. "We stayed there until they were safely off the turnpike."

There were others: The wounded stray dog in Cozumel, Mexico (they convinced a local doctor to treat it with human medicine). The young pigeon that tumbled out of its nest twenty-five feet up in an overpass (they convinced local firemen to take it back up on a ladder). The tiny toad struggling not to get swept away by waves crashing into a parking lot during a storm (Charlie braved the waves, scooped up the toad, and found it a safe place on the other side of the boardwalk).

One April afternoon, Charlie and RoseAnn took a walk along the waterfront in downtown Manhattan. They noticed a group of people gathered at the guardrail, pointing at something in the water. A thirty-foot-long humpback whale had been spotted in the waters beneath the Verrazano-Narrows Bridge and was heading away from the open sea. This wasn't good news for the whale. The whale ran the risk of getting hit by a boat or caught in netting. Unless it headed out to sea, it wouldn't survive.

Charlie and RoseAnn joined the group and watched as the Coast Guard set up a perimeter around the whale. They tried to shield it from ships, but there was no way to steer it away from the harbor—it was up to the whale to do that. The people watching decided to try to will the whale back out to sea. They all focused very hard and sent the whale a message.

For a long while the whale wouldn't budge. Then suddenly it began to head in the right direction, away from the perimeter and toward the open waters south of Coney Island. With one great, final leap forward, the whale pushed away from the harbor and disappeared beneath the surface, on its way to safety.

And the people on shore?

They didn't cheer. Everyone was quiet. They sensed that they had all been part of something magical. "We stood quietly on the shore," says Charlie, "and imagined the whale swimming back home."

Then there was the tiny little bee.

Charlie and RoseAnn were strolling along the boardwalk at Jones Beach when they noticed a bee on the ground. One of its minuscule legs was caught between two planks of wood on the boardwalk. "You could see the bee was trying to yank its leg out and free itself," RoseAnn said. "I don't know how someone hadn't stepped on it already."

RoseAnn got down on her hands and knees and gently pulled on one of the planks until the bee was free. "But he didn't fly away, because he was too exhausted," she recalled. "I slid him onto a tissue, and we took him to a garden and put him near the flowers. Soon enough he started buzzing around the flowers."

During my reading with Charlie and RoseAnn I saw an image of a cruise ship and a pigeon. I had no idea what it meant, but I mentioned it in our reading. Later I would learn the story of the pigeon on the ship.

The couple was on a European cruise when they noticed a pigeon walking on the deck. They wondered what it was doing in the middle of the North Sea and stayed with it until it flew away. Two hours later, they retired below deck to their cabin. When they opened the door, they saw the pigeon on their bed!

Their room had a balcony; they must have left the balcony door open. There had to be a thousand cabins on that boat, but somehow the pigeon had found theirs.

They got some dinner rolls, scraped off the seeds, and made a little dish of food for the pigeon on the balcony. The pigeon ate the seeds and found a comfortable spot to rest. She stayed on their balcony until the ship docked in its next port, Amsterdam. Then she flew away.

Before she did, Charlie had noticed a small tag around one of her legs. It had a series of numbers on the tag they recognized as a phone number. The number was from the Netherlands, and when they got to Amsterdam Charlie dialed it. "We reached someone who connected us to the owner of the pigeon," Charlie told me. "It was a racing pigeon, and it was supposed to fly across the North Sea and end up in France. I guess it needed a little breather, so it wound up on our ship. The owner was so happy to hear from us and to know the pigeon was safe."

───

My reading with Charlie and RoseAnn was one of the densest readings I've ever done. So much love and so many messages poured through the open pathway, I could hardly keep up. A few animals came through more clearly than others. Shadow, their first dog together, was one of them. But I also got specific information about an animal that hadn't crossed yet: one of their beloved cats.

"You have a cat right now who is having a lot of trouble walking," I said. "He had a stroke and he is very sick. But he is not ready to leave you just yet. He wants to stay. So you should wait, because in two weeks he'll be able to walk. And I see a timeline stretching seven months, which means he will stay with you another seven months."

Charlie and RoseAnn were taken aback. Their beloved cat Reggie had indeed just had a stroke. He was barely able to walk at all, and they were all but certain his days were numbered. "He couldn't even stand up," RoseAnn told me later. "We had to lift him up just to get him into a box of cat litter. Honestly, we were thinking it was time to put him down." But since the Other Side said to wait two weeks, they waited. Two weeks later, Reggie strolled into their bedroom like nothing was wrong. Then he ran and cuddled with them. And he stayed with them another seven months.

I had another reading with Charlie and RoseAnn after Reggie crossed, and this time he came through, too.

"Reggie is telling me he can't believe that now he gets to be up on the bed with you," I told them. "He can't believe his luck, and he is so happy about it."

RoseAnn laughed and confirmed they'd never let Reggie sleep with them, because if they let one cat on the bed, they'd have to let them all on.

I've had a few more readings with Charlie and RoseAnn since then, and every time I've been flooded by love and thanks from the Other Side. All the animals they rescued and saved over the last thirty years—the cats and dogs and sparrows and toads and pigeons and ducklings and even the tiny bee—have come through with waves of love and gratitude. Charlie and RoseAnn have devoted their lives to helping and loving the weak and wounded creatures among us, and for that the Other Side is bursting with appreciation.

My readings for Charlie and RoseAnn have taught me a great deal. They reinforced my understanding of the importance of our free will. The choices we make—particularly every act of kindness—are greatly consequential. Our actions matter. Everything Charlie and RoseAnn have done matters. It matters to the great collective energy of all our souls. It matters because they honored the greatest gift we possess—the infinite capacity to love and heal even the smallest of creatures.

The readings were also meaningful for me because of how deeply RoseAnn and Charlie believe that all living creatures share a consciousness. They believe it was this consciousness that allowed the bee to know their intention, the whale to sense the collective thought energy of the people on shore, and the drivers speeding along on the New Jersey Turnpike to avoid the ducks.

It is this consciousness that survives the physical realm.

Today, Charlie and RoseAnn (both vegetarians, of course) take great comfort in the understanding that their family of animals continues to share a powerful bond of love.

My readings with Charlie and RoseAnn serve as further proof for me that our animals survive on the Other Side, and that our bond with them is unbreakable. I've also seen that while our pets are here, they don't want to leave us. Often I will see multiple doorways for pets to cross, and see that they take the very last doorway. Reggie the cat stuck around for seven months. Another couple I read for was sure their twelve-year-old Chihuahua, LaLa, would have to be put down imminently, but in our reading I saw several doorways, one that month and one in each of the following six months. To their surprise, LaLa stayed with them for six more months—a time that allowed them to celebrate their boundless love for each other.

Animals often come through in my readings with important messages for us here on earth. These messages may have to do with the guilt we feel over an animal's passing. Did we do the right thing by putting them to sleep? Did we do enough to save them? Did we cause them extra suffering? Anyone who's ever loved an animal likely knows this feeling. Recently, I did a reading for a woman, and two dogs came through—a larger retriever and a small terrier. I could see the retriever had just crossed, and I could sense the woman was harboring a terrible sense of guilt.

"He is saying you shouldn't have any guilt about his crossing," I told her. "You did everything right. It was his time to go. And you were with him when he crossed, and he wants to thank you for being so gentle and so loving and for being there with him. There is nothing but love, love, love coming from this dog for you."

The woman burst into tears. She told me that when the retriever got sick she faced a difficult choice—she could authorize an operation that had a small chance of helping, or she could put him to sleep. She wanted to do everything in her power to help him, but the risky operation didn't feel right because his illness was so far along. She decided not to go ahead with it and had him put to rest.

Almost instantly she feared she'd made the wrong choice, that she hadn't done enough for her dog, and that at the moment of his greatest need she had let him down. She didn't think she could ever forgive herself.

When we had our reading, her beloved dog's message came through clearly—*I am okay.* I saw that the retriever had paired up with her childhood pet, a little terrier, on the Other Side. He was safe, he was happy, and he wasn't in any pain. Most important, he was grateful to her for her love.

"You didn't make a 'wrong' choice, because all the choices you made were made with love," I told her. "Your deep, abiding love for your dog is what he took with him when he crossed. He took nothing but love."

The woman told me she felt a great burden had been lifted. All the love she had showered on her dog when he was here was coming back to her, just when she needed it most.

The Other Side shows us that when our animals cross they are safe, happy, and pain-free, romping through fields, flying through skies, swimming through reefs, and thanking us for all the love we gave them while they were here.

The message from the Other Side is clear as can be: Our animals are alive. They are waiting for us. We will see them again.

21

Two Meteors

MY PRIVATE READINGS were becoming richer and deeper as my confidence grew and my techniques improved. Each reading was an education. I was learning that nothing in the universe happens by accident: that every person we meet has something to teach us or to learn from us; that the Other Side looks over us with great love and purpose.

I also became aware that while most of those who come to me for readings are believers in the Other Side, many are not. Some are religious and believe in heaven. Some accept there is a heaven but don't believe there is any way for us to connect to it. Some are deeply spiritual and believe in a unifying, universal force. Some come to me fully expecting to contact loved ones who have passed. But some of those I read for are decidedly not believers.

One of them was a man named Jim Calzia.

Jim is a scientist—a geologist. He was born in California and raised on the edge of the Mojave Desert, and as a kid he played near dry hills and rocky outcrops that captured his imagination. He got a Ph.D. in geology and worked for the U.S. Geological Survey for thirty-eight years, mapping mineral deposits, analyzing isotopes, and determining the origin and evolution of rare earth elements. He found real beauty in the dirt and the rocks and the scrub brush, but he also found a kind of certainty.

To Jim, the earth was solid—firm, tactile, substantial. It was his job to understand the nature of that solidity. He believed in what he could hold in his hand: a chunk of titanite, or zircon, or monazite, or some other sturdy mineral on which his reality was built.

His faith, his rock, was his wife, Kathy.

Jim first met Kathy when they were seniors at Culver City High School. A week before the big Backwards Dance, the dance where the girls got to ask out the guys, Kathy—pretty, popular, outgoing—pulled Jim aside. "Would you go to the Backwards Dance with me?" she asked. They were seventeen and would be together for the next forty-five years.

They were in college when they married. They built a beautiful life together in California, Jim as a geologist, Kathy as a nurse educator in the school district. They had three sons, Scott, Kevin, and Chris. In 1994, Jim got the scare of his life when Kathy was diagnosed with breast cancer. She was hospitalized for a month and needed experimental therapy. Their son Kevin's senior prom fell during his mom's hospital stay, so Kevin and his date scrubbed up, put on surgical gowns, and spent most of their prom night in Kathy's room. Jim was there, too, but then, he was always there.

The therapy worked, and Kathy pulled through.

Everything was fine until 2009, the year Kathy retired. Jim was planning his retirement around Kathy's—their idea was to retire together, remodel their house, and spend their golden years there.

But just a few days after retiring, Kathy came down with a case of pneumonia. She'd battled pneumonia before, but this time, instead of getting better, she got sicker. Kathy admitted herself to the hospital. Jim went with her, not thinking for a moment it was anything but a precautionary visit.

Her symptoms wouldn't go away. Doctors realized that her immune system had been compromised by the experimental therapy years before and now it was failing her. Tests showed that Kathy had the rare H1N1 virus—swine flu. She was rushed to intensive care and intubated. She could no longer speak.

Still, Jim had faith that she would recover and be okay. Kathy had fought battles like this before, and she had always won; she was a fighter. For the next week Jim rarely left her side, though she was sedated all the time. Kathy had to have several blood transfusions, and Jim knew how much she hated needles, so he could barely stand to watch when the nurses came in and stuck her. But he knew the transfusions were necessary, and he knew his wife would soldier on.

After five days in the hospital, the nurses gave Kathy what they called a "sedation vacation"—a temporary reduction in sedation so she would be lucid for a while. Kathy's sons gathered around her as she gained consciousness for the first time in days. She couldn't talk because of the tube, but she could point to the letters on an alphabet chart. She wanted her hairbrush and comb, and she wanted to be sure the flowers in the hanging baskets on the side of the garage were being watered.

When the nurses put Kathy under sedation again, the boys went home, but two days later, a nurse told Jim that Kathy's heart was racing at 160 beats a minute. Jim knew Kathy was fighting hard. It was only when the doctor approached him one night in the waiting room that he grew scared.

"I think it might be time to let her go," the doctor said.

Let her go? Let Kathy go? The thought had never crossed his

mind. Not for a second had he contemplated life without Kathy. Let her go? What did that even mean? How can you let go of someone who means everything to you? Jim was terrified.

On her eighth day in intensive care, Kathy's heartbeat started to fade. It was 4:00 a.m. when a nurse explained that they were having trouble getting a transfusion needle into her arm.

"Don't do it," Jim found himself saying. "Don't give her any more needles."

The nurse said there wasn't much time. Jim called his sons and told them to hurry to the hospital. Each had only a few moments to say goodbye. One by one they stroked her arm and kissed her on the cheek. Then Jim bent over Kathy's bed, took her in his arms, and held her.

"I am so proud of you," he whispered. "I know you did the very best you could. I love you, Kathy."

Jim felt a hand on his shoulder. It was his son Scott.

"Dad," Scott said, "she's gone."

Nothing helped to ease Jim's grief. It was profound, bottomless. He kept Kathy's belongings just as they'd always been. He spent most of his time in darkness. He didn't answer calls, didn't allow friends to come by and visit. He's not sure exactly what he did in those dire, desperate months; there are only flickers of memory.

He remembers that he spent the first Christmas without Kathy with his son Kevin and his daughter-in-law Maren and her family. He remembers that at precisely 11:00 a.m. Christmas Day, just about everyone who had known and loved Kathy—even friends as far away as Finland—lit a candle and held it aloft in her memory. But other than that, the months after Kathy passed are a blur, too painful and sad to recall.

He might have spent years like that—maybe even the rest of

his life—but one day he developed a migraine headache. He'd never had one, though Kathy used to get them from time to time. On this day, Jim saw blinding flashes of light and felt a crippling pain in his temple. He fell on his bed and held his head. The migraine made him think of Kathy, and he had a kind of epiphany in that moment.

Kathy would not want this, he thought. She had taken care of him. Together they had built a life, and now, he realized, he was squandering it all.

Jim got a little better after that. He and Kathy had begun the renovation of their home before she passed. Jim now picked up where they'd left off, and he made sure every last detail was exactly the way Kathy had wanted it to be. He was about to have a new electric stove installed when the electrician who'd been working with them objected.

"No, no, no, Kathy talked to me about that," he said. "She wanted a gas stove. A gourmet gas stove. She had a stove with red knobs all picked out."

Jim put in the stove that Kathy had chosen.

Not long after, Jim was returning home from a family reunion, driving down Highway 101 near Shell Beach. He saw something flash into his vision. He looked up through the windshield and into the dark night sky and saw two meteors streaking down toward the beach. They were incredibly bright and fast, and as they hurtled to earth Jim braced for a shock wave. He looked back at the road for a moment, then looked for the meteors again, but they were gone. The sky was quiet. It was almost as if he'd imagined the whole thing.

That night, Jim visited Kathy's brother and asked if he'd heard anything about the two giant meteors over Shell Beach. Kathy's brother hadn't, and neither had anyone else Jim asked.

A few weeks later, Jim got a call from his son Kevin.

"There's something I think you need to see," Kevin said.

Kevin sent Jim a video of a reading his wife Maren had had with a psychic medium. That psychic medium was me.

As it happens, the reading I had with Maren took place a few hours after Jim saw the meteors.

"Just watch it," Kevin said. "Trust me."

Jim and his son Scott watched the reading together. Almost immediately, Jim noticed that I was making gestures with my hands that were familiar to him. They were Kathy's gestures.

He leaned forward and listened as I described a series of family events and births and happenings in precisely the way his wife would have described them.

"How can she know this stuff?" he wondered. "Why is she acting like Kathy?"

Jim listened as Kathy talked—through me—for the next sixty minutes.

Then, toward the end of the reading, Maren asked me, "Has Kathy ever tried to contact Jim since she passed?"

Jim held his breath. He couldn't process what he was seeing and hearing. Yet he needed to hear the answer.

"Oh, yes," I told Maren. "She has tried and tried and tried. But every time she gets close he goes deeper and deeper into the darkness. She doesn't want to hurt him, but she keeps trying. She has tried everything. She says she has even tried meteors!"

Jim jumped to his feet.

"I need to see this woman myself," he said.

It had been nearly a year since Kathy's passing when I had my reading with Jim. We met at Maren's parents' home in Huntington Station on Long Island. I knew nothing about him other than that his wife had died a year earlier. He was clearly nervous. He was tall, with a full head of graying hair and eyes that smiled when he smiled. He wasn't young, yet he seemed boyish. His face was open and friendly, and his energy was adventurous yet grounded. He was someone you would want to spend time with. But I could also feel how deeply sad he was.

We sat down and I read his energy for a minute or two. Then, very quickly, I felt his wife step through. She showed me a very clear image.

"Your wife is showing me your house is in disarray," I said. "The walls are knocked out, the floors are torn up, the ceiling is being lowered. Everything is upside down."

Jim shook his head and smiled. He was in the middle of the remodel. The walls, the floors, the ceiling—everything was just as I described it.

"I'm also seeing something like a stove," I said. "A stove with red knobs."

Jim began to cry.

Kathy gave me detail after detail that validated her presence. She showed me a handprint on a wall.

"She is showing me this handprint, and she is saying she sees you touching this wall in the kitchen," I said.

Jim shook his head and smiled.

"The kitchen was her favorite room," he explained. "Every morning when I go in, I touch the wall for her. Every single morning."

"She is acknowledging that," I said. "She is touching you back."

Kathy showed me something in a drawer—a small jar of nail polish.

"Kathy is laughing about it," I told Jim. "She is laughing and saying, 'Tease him about why he needs my nail polish.'"

Jim was laughing now, too. "She's right," he said. "I saved her nail polish. I keep it in the garage. It's the same shade of red as my car. So I use it whenever I need to touch up the car."

Something about Jim keeping his wife's nail polish was incredibly touching to me. The nail polish had been hers, and now it was his, and they used it in wildly different ways, but for both of them it was indispensable. The tiny jar was a stitch in the fabric of their lives together—one that continued to bind them across the reaches of time and space.

My reading with Jim showed me how persistently our loved ones try to communicate with us from the Other Side—and how we need to change our perception of the world in order for them to come through.

Jim and I spoke for more than an hour. Kathy came through with many other intimate details. Jim kept shaking his head, wondering how I could know such things. But of course I didn't know them. I was only passing them along for Kathy.

When the reading was over, Jim seemed shaken. He stood up and took a couple of deep breaths, and then he hugged me.

"It felt like I was having a conversation with Kathy," he said. "I didn't think I'd ever be able to talk to her again."

Jim asked to set up another reading, but I knew that wasn't necessary.

"You don't need me," I said. "You don't need me to talk to Kathy. She is everywhere around you. All you have to do is be aware of your surroundings. When something happens, pay attention."

Jim went home, bought a scrapbook, and started writing down everything that struck him as out of the ordinary. He wrote about the rosebush that Kathy's colleagues had given her when she retired, how they'd planted it in the front yard, and how it started blooming just after Kathy passed away. Those roses are bigger, brighter, and more magnificent than any other flowers in the garden.

He wrote about the day of their wedding anniversary, and how he and Scott went to dinner in a restaurant they hadn't been to in a long time. The first thing that jumped off the menu was an entrée called honey walnut prawns—that had been Kathy's favorite meal.

He wrote about the beautiful white dove that flew into the garage while he was working on his car, and how the dove landed and looked at him, and how he had looked back, and how they stared at each other for what felt like the longest time, until the dove flew off. Jim watched it go and said aloud, though only he could hear, "That was Kathy."

Jim even went back to work, accepting a position as a geologist emeritus and continuing his research projects in California's Death Valley. There are no trees in Death Valley, no hills and nothing green. To him, though, Death Valley is a place of beauty and certainty, full of rocks and minerals he can hold in his hands. But in the bare brown landscape, Jim found something as real to him as anything else on earth: he found Kathy.

"I feel like she is here," Jim says. "I feel like she is always around me and we are always in communication. I feel like our love is the same as it's ever been."

Jim believes in something science cannot prove—that one day he and Kathy will be together again. The reading opened his eyes and his heart.

"I can see a scenario where Kathy and I will be reunited," he says. "I have the tools I need now to go on. To live how Kathy would want me to live."

Jim no longer needs two meteors streaking through the sky. All he needs is a simple white dove. Or a dish of honey walnut prawns. Or anything, really, that reminds him of Kathy and of the love they share.

"I think Kathy would be proud of me," Jim says. "In fact, I know she is."

And when Jim finally finished renovating the house he shared with his wife, he put an elegant, engraved bronze plaque on the front door: KATHY'S HOUSE.

22

Windbridge

MY QUEST TO DISCOVER where I fit in the world never waned. As a teacher, I urged my students to be relentless in their search for knowledge, and as a psychic medium, I put that lesson into practice. There were big questions I still needed to answer.

Phran and Bob Ginsberg suggested that I look into the Windbridge Institute for Applied Research in Human Potential, an organization made up of scientists dedicated to researching phenomena currently unexplained within traditional scientific disciplines. Windbridge, based in Arizona, was cofounded by Dr. Julie Beischel, who is also the director of research. Two of the Forever Family Foundation mediums, Joanne Gerber and Doreen Molloy, were also already Windbridge research mediums. I loved the idea of being able to use my abilities not only to help those in grief but also to further scientific investigation.

The mission statement of Windbridge stated that the organization "is concerned with asking, 'What can we do with the potential that exists within our bodies, minds, and spirits?' Can we heal each other? Ourselves? . . . Can we communicate with our loved ones who have passed?"

I learned that Windbridge offers a rigorous screening and certification of people with mediumistic abilities. It is an eight-step process that includes a quintuple-blind reading. The process was designed to eliminate any possibility of outside factors—cold readings, participant bias, experimenter cuing, even telepathy—influencing the results. In a quintuple-blind reading, the people monitoring the experiment are blinded to all information. They know nothing about the discarnates (the term used for the deceased loved ones), nor which mediums performed which readings, or even which readers were intended for which sitters.

For years I'd yearned to know what accounted for my unique abilities and what the implications were for me personally, psychologically, and physiologically. It seemed that I might find some answers at Windbridge. I emailed Dr. Beischel and told her I wanted to take the test.

Dr. Beischel earned a B.S. in environmental sciences and a Ph.D. in pharmacology and toxicology from the University of Arizona. While she was still a student, her mother committed suicide, after which she visited a psychic medium. She found the reading to be meaningful and became curious about the paranormal.

Dr. Beischel responded quickly to my inquiry and had me complete a questionnaire that covered my personal history, education level, health issues, specific psychic abilities, and the like. Next I submitted to a personality test based on the Myers-Briggs Type Indicator, a clinical screening that measures extroversion, agreeableness, and other personality traits. The third step was an interview with two of the institute's certified mediums. Their job was to determine what my motives were, if I would be a good teammate, whether I was interested in furthering the science of parapsychology—things like that. I had wonderful conversations with the mediums who interviewed me. In fact, as I listened to myself respond to their questions, I was surprised by some of my own answers. It was as if the Other Side was guiding me through this part of the process.

"Where do you see yourself in five years, in terms of the mediumistic work you do?" one of the mediums asked me. I heard myself say that my commitment to my work as a medium was going to take the front seat in life and that I was excited because I would be working with a team of light on the Other Side—children who had crossed—to get the messages out here that life continues on the Other Side and that there is no death. I saw it as my mission to help people live the best versions of our lives in the here and now. I spoke about wanting to be part of Windbridge so that the way in which mediumship works could be explored. It gave me strength and confidence to talk to other mediums who were on the same page and understood what it was like to live life with the knowledge that the Other Side is real. We all understood the same truths. I smiled when I learned I had passed the interview portion.

The next part of the process was an interview with Dr. Beischel, conducted over the phone. She asked me about my process and also questioned my intent—why I wanted to submit to Windbridge's certification and how I used and intended to use my gift. After about a half hour, she informed me that I would be moving on to the next stage: Step Five.

In this part of the process, I would be asked to remotely read two volunteer sitters chosen by Windbridge researchers, and to try to connect, for each sitter, with a specific loved one who had crossed. Although I didn't know it at the time, the discarnates who'd been selected were intentionally very different—a young person and an elderly one, for instance—to discourage general readings that could apply to both sitters.

I would not be given the sitter's name or that person's relationship to the deceased. All I would be given was the first name of the departed. The researcher who selected the sitters would give the names of the deceased to Dr. Beischel. Then Dr. Beischel would call me, give me the name of one of the deceased, set a timer for fifteen minutes, and ask me specific questions about the deceased's personality, physical appearance, and interests, plus how he or she died.

Neither Dr. Beischel nor I knew anything about the departed soul or the sitter. What's more, the sitter would know nothing about me and wouldn't learn the results of my reading until later. All I'd have to go on was a name.

This protocol ensured that the only way I could get information was from the deceased. Would this work? Would the deceased know where to find me when the call came? Would I be able to connect without the sitter present on the phone—or even aware that the reading was taking place? What had I agreed to? I turned to the only people I knew who would understand the anxiety I was feeling: Kim and Bobbi. I described the process to them.

"It will work," Kim assured me.

"The Other Side will know exactly where to find you to get their messages through," Bobbi said.

On the appointed day, I was nervous. I sat on my bed, waiting for the call from Dr. Beischel.

"The deceased person you are to contact is named Mary," Dr. Beischel stated matter-of-factly. "Please start by telling me what she looked like and how she crossed."

We were off. I didn't have time to be nervous because all at once I felt an incredible flood of information come through. Suddenly I was describing Mary, identifying her connection to the sitter, drawing a portrait of her and her life. She showed me that she was about five feet eight inches tall, with blond hair and light eyes, and close to eighty years old when she crossed. She showed me hobbies: gardening, reading, riding a bike. She told me she had been married and had two children. She brought me to her chest area as to cause of death, and I felt a shortness of breath. She showed me a hospital. I got the impression she had been ill for a while and had crossed through an illness, not as the result of an accident. Even as it was happening, I could hardly believe all this information was coming through so easily.

After fifteen minutes Dr. Beischel thanked me. She told me that one week later at the same time she would call me for the second reading. I hung up the phone in a bit of a daze, left my bedroom, and went into the kitchen, where my kids were playing quietly. My mom had been babysitting while I took the call.

"How did it go?" she asked.

"It was an amazing experience," I said. "The minute I heard the name, I felt someone come through and give me all this information. I didn't know if I'd be able to do it without a sitter present, but the Other Side knew how to find me."

"That's wonderful," my mom said. "It sounds like it went great."

"Well, the way I see it, there are only two options: either I'm delusional and just made up an entire life story or it worked."

A week later Dr. Beischel called me for the second reading. While things had seemed to go well last time, I was still pretty nervous. Dr. Beischel told me the deceased's name was Jennifer. Just as before, the information poured out. The words and images came so fast I felt like I was dictating a novel. This time, I saw a young woman, likely in her late twenties. She showed me brown curly hair and green eyes. She showed me that she liked music and had played the flute. I saw she had family here: a mom, a dad, a brother, a sister. She singled out a family member—her mother. I felt like she wanted to tell her mom she was okay. She showed me a crossing from an illness that had progressed faster than the family thought it would. There was no time for a proper goodbye, because she had been unconscious when she crossed.

The rush of information was exhilarating. At the same time, because I wasn't getting any feedback, I had no idea if what I was saying had any relevance. Neither did Dr. Beischel. At the end of fifteen minutes Dr. Beischel thanked me and told me to expect the results within a few weeks.

Dr. Beischel transcribed the tapes of my two readings, formatted them into lists of items, and emailed them to a Windbridge researcher—not the one who'd originally interviewed the sitters. Furthermore, she redacted the names of the deceased, so the researcher didn't know which reading was for which sitter.

The researcher then mailed the two sets of results to the sitters. The sitters, not knowing which reading was intended for them, rated each of the roughly 100 items in each list as to how well it applied to their loved one. They scored each statement from 0 to 6 for accuracy. A statement that made sense and required little interpretation received a high score. A statement that needed a lot of interpretation to make it relevant scored low. For instance, if something was clearly on the money, it might get a 6. If the statement was true but was about a different deceased relative, it might get a 2. Statements that bore no relevance got a 0. The numerical grades of each statement would be added up into an aggregate score. At the end of the scoring, each sitter chose which reading he or she believed was his or hers.

In order for a psychic medium to pass this portion of the test, each sitter had to identify the correct reading for his or her deceased relative and score it at 3.5 or higher. The score for the reading that wasn't for that person had to come in at a 2.0 or lower.

About two weeks after the second reading, just as I was setting the table for dinner, Dr. Beischel called. I shushed my kids and quickly took the phone into my bedroom, my heart pounding. We made small talk for a minute before an awkward silence set in. I felt like one of my own students in the dreadful moment before being handed the results of a test. I wondered if she was stalling because she had bad news.

"So, I have your test results," Dr. Beischel finally said. "You passed this portion."

I felt a surge of relief and got a bit emotional, but held it in check because I knew those two readings were only the first stage of this part of the process.

The readings I'd passed were called sitter-absent readings. In the next round, I would read for the same sitters and try to connect with the same deceased relatives, but this time the sitter would be on the call, along with Dr. Beischel. Dr. Beischel would not identify the sitter, the sitter's relationship to the departed, or even the sitter's gender—just the name of the one who had crossed. The sitter was also instructed to remain silent during the first ten minutes of the reading.

About a week later, at the designated time, Dr. Beischel called and reported that she had the sitter on the line.

"Sitter, please push a button on your phone to acknowledge that you are ready," Dr. Beischel instructed. I heard a tone—the sitter was on the call.

Dr. Beischel told me that I was once again to connect with Mary.

"Please begin," she said.

Right away, the Other Side gave me the sitter's name, Lisa, and her occupation—she was a nurse. I received images that informed me that Mary was Lisa's grandmother and that she'd been a mother figure to her. The next ten minutes went by with barely a pause to catch my breath—that's how quickly the information came through. I felt the same rush of exhilaration I'd felt in the earlier readings.

After ten minutes, Dr. Beischel instructed the sitter to say a single word—"hello"—and then to respond to the information I shared with "yes," "no," "maybe," "sort of," or "I don't know." In this segment of the reading, the interaction segment, even more came through. Lisa's grandmother began to tell me about Lisa's life. She was single but had a little dog. She was hardworking and had put herself through school. She had been closer with her grandmother than with her biological mother. Lisa's grandmother thanked her for taking care of her when she was ill, and for being there when she crossed.

At the end of the reading, Lisa thanked me. She said it was wonderful to be able to connect with her grandmother again. I felt elated that I had gotten the sitter's relationship to the deceased right and even happier that Mary had given me Lisa's name! I was grateful that Mary had done such a good job communicating her information.

A week later, I had my second sitter-present reading. Dr. Beischel asked me to connect with Jennifer again. Instantly the Other Side let me know the sitter on the call was a mother whose daughter, Jennifer, had crossed. Then I heard the daughter singing a peculiar song: the Oscar Mayer jingle. *Oh, I wish I was an Oscar Mayer wiener* . . .

I saw the word *Massachusetts*, and then Jennifer showed me a beautifully clear lake with what looked like crystals bouncing off the surface on a warm summer day. I saw majestic, towering pine trees. I recounted all of this to my silent sitter.

In the second portion of the reading, when the sitter could talk, I learned that she was the mother of a daughter who had crossed. Later in the call, once the reading was over, the sitter asked Dr. Beischel if she could quickly tell me one thing. She wanted to confirm why the Oscar Mayer jingle was so important to her.

"I have a photo of my daughter from one Halloween," she told me. "She is dressed as the Oscar Mayer wiener. She loved that song. She sang it all the time."

A few weeks later Dr. Beischel forwarded me an email from this sitter, whose name, I learned, was Jeanne. She wanted to validate something else that had come up in our reading. "I live in the woods on a lake," she wrote. "And just when you said the word 'lake,' I was looking out at the lake. And just when you said there was sunshine on the lake, the sun burst through the clouds and shone down on the lake. It gave me goose bumps on top of goose bumps."

What a remarkable moment. Jeanne was looking at the very lake that her daughter was describing to me. The lake and their house, she told me, were surrounded by pine trees. Jeanne took from this that her daughter was right there beside her, and she had carefully described the lake to let her mother know she was with her at that moment.

After the readings, the sitters scored the information I provided. Days went by, and though I felt confident, I was anxious to get confirmation that I'd passed this part of the test.

On Halloween night, just after I'd returned from trick-or-treating with my kids and while I was still wearing my black witch's hat and cape, I checked my email and saw a message from Dr. Beischel in my inbox. My hands shook. I knew the email held the results of this last step. There was to be no phone call, no ceremony, no trumpets or confetti. Just an email that would say either *Congratulations, you're moving on to the next step* or *Thanks, but you're done.*

"Garrett, this is it. The email is here," I said.

"Open it," he said.

The kids chimed in. "Open it!"

I waited another moment before opening the email. Every time I went to click on it, my hand involuntarily pulled away from the keyboard. Finally I took a deep breath and opened the email.

"I am pleased to inform you that you have successfully passed the initial five screening steps," Dr. Beischel wrote. *"I am happy to invite you to continue with the remaining screening and training steps. Congratulations!"*

My eyes filled with tears. I turned to Garrett and the kids, unable to talk.

"What?" he asked, concerned. "Did you pass?"

"Yes," I squeaked, as I dissolved in tears. My family gathered around me and enveloped me in a hug.

"Why is Mommy crying if she passed the test?" Hayden asked.

"Because she's happy," Garrett said, and hugged me tighter.

Adding to my emotions, though, was something that no one knew, something I hadn't told anyone. I had made a promise the day I agreed to be tested at the Windbridge Institute—a promise to myself, and to the Other Side. I agreed that if I passed this test, I would never again question my abilities. Either I was a medium, communication with the dead was real, and the deceased would know how to find me and talk to me and give me valid information, or all of that wasn't true.

But now I knew. The Other Side had done its part.

Now it was time for me to do mine.

The last line of Dr. Beischel's email read, *"Please let me know if you would like to continue participating in the WCRM screening process."*

I decided that I would honor my connection to the Other Side and dedicate myself to developing my abilities further and using them to help as many people as I could. This included becoming a research medium and allowing scientists to study me to learn more about my abilities. I wrote back immediately saying yes, I wanted to keep going. There were three more steps for me to complete—mediumship research training, human research subjects training, and grief training. The training was designed to teach me the history of mediumship and science over the past century, educate me on the ethics of agreeing to be studied by scientists at Windbridge, and pass along the institute's insights about how best to help sitters during and after a reading. After completing those steps, I received a certificate in the mail. I was officially a Windbridge Certified Research Medium. I am one of nineteen such Certified Research Mediums in the country. The institute's certification meant that I could participate in Windbridge experiments and events and help the institute further its research into the paranormal. I was elated. I could work with Windbridge on the scientific aspects and with the Forever Family Foundation in helping the bereaved. I felt connected to the Other Side and honored to be part of a team of light.

I wrote to Phran with the news that Windbridge had certified me and thanked her for steering me toward Dr. Beischel. I called Kim and Bobbi and encouraged them to test for Windbridge—and I'm happy to report that Kim, too, became a Windbridge Certified Medium. (Bobbi missed the testing by one month—it was already closed by the time she contacted them.)

Eventually I learned the scores from my second round of readings—the sitter-present readings. One sitter scored 90 percent of my statements segment as accurate. The other sitter scored the accuracy of her reading at 95 percent.

What did all that mean? I wondered what conclusions Dr. Beischel could draw from the testing.

"As a scientist, I cannot definitively declare that mediums communicate with the dead," Dr. Beischel said. "But what I can say is the data is leaning that way. Science is heading in that direction. The science is catching up. My data supports that communication with the consciousness of those who are dead is possible."

But for me, the certificate also meant something else. It meant I'd graduated to the next level of my journey.

PART THREE

23

The Canarsie Pier

IN NOVEMBER 2010, I got a phone call out of the blue from my friend Anthony. He asked me to do a reading for his friend Maria as soon as possible. He told me that she was in a desperate situation: Her father had been missing for ten days. No one knew where he was or if he was still alive.

I arranged to call Maria the next day. When I reached her she was driving. She asked for a minute to pull over, and in the silence I could feel her sadness and confusion. I could also immediately sense someone pushing through from the Other Side. A father figure. This was not what I wanted to see. This wasn't what I wanted to tell Maria. It was going to be hard, but I had no choice. I had to honor what I was getting from the Other Side.

"Maria, there's something I have to tell you," I said when she was in place, as gently as I could. "I have a father figure coming

Some of the names of the people mentioned in this chapter have been changed to disguise their identities.

through for you on the Other Side. He says to tell you his name is John."

I soon learned that my reading was taking place in the middle of an open police investigation.

===

The investigation had begun almost two weeks earlier, on November 4, 2010, a cold and rainy day. A man named John, age seventy-two, spent the morning at home in Queens, New York. His wife, Mary, was with him. Around 12:30 p.m. Mary prepared to leave for her job working with special education students. She wasn't feeling well that morning, and John told her he was worried that she hadn't eaten lunch.

"Don't worry," she told him, "I'll eat when I get back."

Then Mary said goodbye and left.

On another day, John would likely have stayed home for lunch, or maybe gone for a walk. But on that day John went to the front door and stepped into the freezing rain. He wasn't wearing a coat, just a sweatsuit. He didn't take his phone, his keys, his wallet, or any money. He didn't even take his inhaler, which he used for his emphysema.

When Mary came home two hours later, she called out for John, but there was no answer. She looked all over the house, but he wasn't there. When she found his keys and wallet, a terrible feeling of dread swept over her. Her ordinary day was ordinary no more.

===

Family meant everything to John. He had worked hard to provide for his wife and three children. He had been a landscaper by trade, and he grew tomatoes in his backyard garden. Those who knew him described him as a straight shooter and a gentle soul.

When he retired, he helped his daughter Maria take care of her infant son.

But in the year before he walked away, John began to change. He became more introverted, subdued. He was quick to anger and could be irritable. Sometimes he would bring up an old grievance—something that had troubled him decades before— and complain about it as if it had just happened. Maria took him to a neurologist, who diagnosed John as being in the early stages of Alzheimer's disease.

Under the watchful eye of his wife and children, John started on Alzheimer's medication, but it left him listless and closed off. His family struggled to help him. "We had been in such denial," Maria explained. "We thought his symptoms were just the symptoms of old age. We were just at the beginning of the process, trying to figure out what was best for him. But we could see he was declining."

Then on November 4, John walked away. When his wife couldn't find him at home, she got in her car and drove around the neighborhood searching for him. After twenty minutes she pulled over and called her daughter.

"Your father is missing," she said.

"What do you mean he's missing?" Maria said.

"He's gone. He's just gone. His keys and his wallet are at home, but he's gone."

"Okay," Maria said, quickly gathering her thoughts. "Let's call the police."

That night all three of John's children drove around Queens looking for him. The next day they walked the streets, talking to shop owners and posting flyers. "We walked into every store on the boulevard, from one end to the other," Maria said. At the very last store, a tanning salon, Maria showed her father's picture to a young cashier.

"Oh, my God," the cashier said. "I saw your father yesterday!"

The cashier had been at the local bakery getting lunch when she saw John outside, asking someone for five dollars. That news gave Maria a glimmer of hope. For the next three days she sat in her parked car across from the bakery, waiting to see if her father would come back.

Meanwhile, a neighborhood search that had begun with a few friends and relatives handing out flyers turned into one of the biggest manhunts in the history of Queens. For almost two weeks, a massive search party that included police on horseback, helicopters, search dogs, TV reporters, and a small army of volunteers canvassed every corner of Queens for any sign of John.

But there were no signs. He had disappeared without a trace.

It was around that time that I got the call from my friend Anthony and arranged my reading with Maria.

When I said her father was coming through from the Other Side, Maria began to cry. I waited for her to collect herself, and then I told her what John was showing me.

On November 4 John had left his home confused and disoriented. Though he had no money, he got on a bus, and later a train. He walked down streets he knew and some he didn't. He went to the bakery and a few other places that had been part of his routine. But he was aimless—he had no destination, no real direction. Then on my reading screen he showed me a sign that read CANARSIE. After that, he showed me water and then a pier. I had no idea what it meant, but I passed it along to Maria.

"That's the Canarsie Pier!" she gasped. "It's in Brooklyn, on the border of Queens. It was my father's favorite place in the world. He used to take us there all the time when we were little."

The six-hundred-foot wooden pier, built behind Canarsie Park along the Belt Parkway in Queens, juts into Jamaica Bay and is a popular spot for fishing—people catch fluke and bluefish in season. John loved to fish there, and when he got older he enjoyed strolling along the wooden planks out toward the water. After John vanished, the Canarsie Pier was one of the first places his family had looked for him, but they found no evidence that he'd been there.

Now John showed me what he'd done when he got to the pier. As gently as I could, I told Maria what I was seeing.

John stopped in Canarsie Park to gather some rocks. He put the rocks into the pockets of his sweatsuit and walked to the end of the pier. It was dark and cold out, and the pier was empty. He lowered himself under the guardrail and slipped into the water.

"Within two minutes of entering the water," I said, "your father drowned."

At the very moment he crossed, though, John had felt a terrible pang of regret.

"He says to tell you he is sorry for what you're going through now, searching for him," I told her. "He thought his body would be found in a day or two, but the currents took him away. He says he is sorry for all the confusion he caused." John showed me two letters, *M* and *A*, and I understood what that meant. "There's no point in searching for his body now," I said. "It won't be found until a month that begins with *Ma*—March or May. The current won't return him before then."

John showed me that he'd killed himself because he was afraid of what was happening to him as a result of dementia. Maria quickly validated this. "He believed he would end up being a burden to his family, and he did not want that to happen," I said. "He didn't want to be an imposition. But then, as soon as he went under, he realized that he had made a terrible mistake."

By killing himself, he had meant to spare his family a great burden. Instead, he realized, he'd cheated them of a great gift.

John's illness, which seemed like a painful, miserable fate, was actually a remarkable opportunity for them to share and deepen the immense, unconditional love they felt for each other. The sicker John got, the more he would need the care and attention of his family—but in the darkness of his illness lay lessons John still needed to learn, and lessons he needed to teach.

Perhaps one of the lessons was patience. Perhaps it was compassion. Perhaps it was unconditional love. Or an understanding of our power to heal, or overcoming our fear of death. John deprived himself and his family of the chance to learn these lessons. He didn't see that the act of caring for him—of offering comfort to someone they felt so richly indebted to—would not diminish his family's love for him but rather enlarge it. He didn't realize that letting his family care for him during the most vulnerable time in his life would give them the chance to revel in their deep, powerful, loving connection.

John's decision to end his life cheated them of this gift.

"He says he's sorry," I told Maria. "He is saying it over and over: 'I am sorry.'"

After our reading, Maria contacted NYPD detective Frank Garcia, who was in charge of her father's missing-person case. Maria gave him the information I'd told her in our reading.

"I need you to search the water," she said. "My father is in the water."

Detective Garcia agreed to help her look for her father. Together they spent five hours on a frigid, rainy day climbing across the jagged rocks that bordered Jamaica Bay. It was so cold Maria's hands and feet were numb, but she kept going—they both did. But in the end, the search was fruitless. Wherever John was, he would not be found just yet.

"I'll let you know if I hear anything," Detective Garcia promised her. "Don't worry, we will find him."

March came and went with no news. Winter gave way to spring.

On the first day of May, Mary called Detective Garcia. "This is when we will find him," she said. "A month with the letters *Ma*."

"We'll be on the lookout," the detective promised.

But the month of May came and went, too, and still nothing.

———

In early June, Detective Garcia got a phone call from the Coast Guard. The Guard forces had been performing exercises on an island in Jamaica Bay when an officer noticed something that had washed up on shore. It was human remains—not a whole body, just a skull. The Coast Guard retrieved the remains and sent them out for DNA testing. It took several days for the results to come back, but when they did they were identified as John's.

"When did you find them?" Detective Garcia asked.

"A few days ago," the Coast Guard officer replied. "In May."

Detective Garcia called Maria and gave her the news. He also explained why the remains had taken so long to surface. When a body goes into the water in the winter, it sinks to the bottom and gets swept away by the tides. When the weather gets warm, the body will likely rise to the surface. The remains of John's body eventually appeared not far from the Canarsie Pier, where he crossed. He had been in those waters all along—he just couldn't be found.

"This has never happened," Detective Garcia told Maria.

"What hasn't happened?"

"This," he said. "The way your psychic gave us the play-by-play for when and where we would find your father. Everything she told you is exactly what happened. I've never seen that before."

But for Maria, it wasn't surprising at all. "I was at peace by the time the detective called," she said. "I already knew my father was in heaven."

John *was* in heaven. Even those who commit suicide go to heaven. There they heal and then continue on their journey of growth and understanding. They try to help their loved ones back on earth heal, too. John was safe and loved in heaven, but he reached out to ask for forgiveness—and to give his family peace of mind.

It was difficult for Maria to forgive him at first. His decision had caused them all such pain. But over time she came to forgive him. She understood why he'd done it. And she knew the love they shared didn't end when he crossed. She knew it would never end.

But what if John had understood these lessons before he slipped into the dark water? What if the whole family had approached his illness as part of a greater design—as a chance for them all to grow and tap into a deep well of love and compassion? Imagine if we could all have that kind of clarity while we're here on earth. Imagine if we could all see illness and adversity as opportunities to expand our love on a soul level.

The truth is, we can achieve this clarity. We simply need to see and appreciate the cords of light and love that bind us, in good times and in bad, in this life and the next. We need to honor the light between us.

John saw this light a moment too late. But now he is sharing the lessons he learned, and through this gift he lives on, and his light shines a path through this world.

24

Solving the Riddle

I DON'T ADVERTISE my services as a psychic medium. It was made clear to me a long time ago that whoever is supposed to have a reading with me will somehow find me. So when my friend John told me that one of his friends, Ken, would be reaching out to me for a reading, I promised I'd get him scheduled as soon as I could.

I read for Ken over the phone. When I first opened to his aura, I immediately saw something very distinct and different—a dazzling array of colors. Like a rainbow, only fuller and way more intense. Colors upon colors upon colors, all of them pure and vibrant and explosive. It was something I'd never experienced before in a reading.

"My God, your aura is magnificent," I said. "It is not a normal aura."

Normally, a person's core aura comes in a range of one to three colors within a circle on my screen. But Ken's aura was gigantic and expansive, with colors swirling not only around the inner circle but outside it, too.

I saw a beautiful green, which signaled a brilliant openness to new ideas. I saw white, the mastery of a soul test. And I saw pink, an expression of his overwhelming love for humanity. There was also an extraordinary bright blue.

"Blue is a sign of nobility of spirit," I told Ken. "This blue suggests that you are here on a much more advanced spiritual level. You are someone who is here to help heal and teach humanity. And the way the blue is linked to the other colors . . . it means your energy is going out to the world, and you are bringing change to others."

Usually I'd spend only a few minutes looking at someone's aura, but with Ken I couldn't help wanting to linger in his beautiful energy.

"You have a very balancing, healing effect on people," I went on. "And above you I see white, and when I see white in someone's aura it always means he or she is mastering a soul test— something his or her soul challenged itself to work on while here on earth. But your soul test wasn't just about you. I see a definite teacher's energy to you, but it expands beyond a normal classroom. You're here on this earth in a physical form on a very advanced spiritual level, and yet there's a humility about you, a humbleness. It's very beautiful. You haven't just mastered your soul test; you're going to help other people master theirs, too. Whatever work you're doing here is going to resonate after you cross and bring about healing and love. Wow.

"I'm sorry to stay in your aura so long," I finally said, "but I don't often see something like this."

When I moved on from Ken's aura, I heard a beautiful chorus of gratitude.

"There are all these thank-yous coming from the Other Side," I said. "It's giving me chills. Somehow you're teaching others about the Other Side. I feel you know more than I do about it. Do you understand?"

Ken told me he did.

"There are children over there who are thanking you for . . . for bringing peace to their parents," I went on. "There are a lot of them, but you're not related to them. It's a thank-you on behalf of all the children—they're thanking you for the work you're doing. When people cross and do their life reviews, they realize how they could have helped people when they were here. With you, it's as if you already have that knowledge, but you're here. You help bring other people to that knowledge. It's very beautiful what I'm seeing. Very beautiful."

A woman began to push through for Ken.

"I am getting that there's an *R* name coming through connected to your grandmother."

"Yes," Ken said. "Her name did begin with an *R*."

"Was it Ruth?"

"Yes!" Ken said.

"She tells me you are a peacemaker," I continued. "She tells me that's a role you've stepped into. I'm supposed to tell you— and I think she brings this up because she was from another country—that one thing you've learned is that we are not from any one particular country. I mean, we came to believe that our nationality was our identity. We can look at ourselves simply as fellow human beings and not be so identified by our nationality, because we are all connected. It's a very advanced way of thinking, a very healing way of thinking, and you are very aware of that, and that's one of the messages you're going to be trying to share."

By then I understood that the man I was reading was on a soul mission—a man whose work was going to resonate long after he crossed and bring love and healing to the world.

Long after the reading, I learned that Ken was Dr. Kenneth Ring, a professor emeritus of psychology at the University of Connecticut and one of the leading scholars in the field of NDEs—near-death experiences. An NDE is described as a mystical or transcendent experience reported by people who have been on the threshold of death. Over the last several decades Ken has established himself as a thoughtful spokesman for the existence of an afterlife. His beautiful book *Lessons from the Light* explores several remarkable stories of NDEs. Its message is that we need not fear death. "What we encounter will be beautiful, more beautiful than words can express," he writes. "Because the truth is, we are connected to another world."

The information that came through in my reading with Ken Ring—that he was somehow helping a great number of people—was validated by what I learned about NDEs. Studies suggest that millions of people worldwide have experienced an NDE. NDEs occur across all countries, ages, and religions. They happen to Christians and Hindus and Muslims, to old people and young, to construction workers and CEOs, to the most devout believers in mystical events and the most skeptical.

This was what the Other Side was showing me about Ken Ring—his work was bringing love, healing, and understanding to millions of people. He was changing the way people perceived existence itself. He was bringing real and meaningful change to the world.

Put simply, Ken Ring was a Light Worker.

Light Worker is the term I use to describe people who are here on this earth to help teach and heal other people. They are people who help others find their gifts and become the best versions of themselves and they, in turn, can then use their light to help others. My reading with Ken was hugely important for me, because it showed me the power a Light Worker has—the power we all have—to bring healing and understanding to the world. And it reinforced the importance of appreciating and exploring our connection to the Other Side—of honoring the light between us.

Despite Ken's work in the science of the afterlife, he'd felt no urge to contact a psychic medium. But then a colleague told him about her first reading and said it had been life-changing. A few days later, by coincidence, another colleague did the same. Within just a few weeks, four colleagues shared their experiences with a psychic medium, and all of them said they were deeply moved by the experience. That's when Ken called me.

The truth was, he did have a reason to see a psychic medium. He was wrestling with a question that had to do with his father, who had crossed when Ken was seventeen. For most of his life, Ken had the feeling his father was still with him. He didn't have visions or hear voices or anything like that—he just felt his father's presence. He felt his father's essence as if he were a force in his life, guiding him. Mostly he still felt his father's love, even though they were separated.

Long before our reading Ken wrote about these feelings in a memoir: "I have always felt my father's love as the primordial fact of my life, even when he was forced to part from me. And when I die, I hope I will have my own confirmation of this feeling when, at last, I may see him once more with his arms outstretched, waiting to welcome me home."

Now, in our reading, Ken wanted to know if what he felt was real.

Several members of Ken's family came through in the reading, all at once, talking over each other, pushing to be heard. His mother came through, and then someone on his mother's side named Mary, who was strong and forceful. Ken said it was his aunt Mary. Then the Other Side brought up someone with a *D* in his name.

"Is there a David here on earth?" I asked.

Ken said his son was named David.

"I'm also getting a Kathryn," I said.

That was the name of Ken's daughter. The Other Side told me about his grandson Max, too.

Ken's father was there, too, but he was staying in the background.

After a while, Ken asked about his father. Only then did the father step forward.

"I feel like he crossed before his time," I said, "Your time together was abbreviated. And I hear an apology for that. He apologizes to you, that's what I'm getting. It's like in a way he was letting you down. As if he crossed without having enough time with you as your father. I am getting the chest area. Something in the chest area. There wasn't even time for a goodbye."

Ken told me that he hadn't been there when his father died of a heart attack.

"Your father is saying, 'I'm sorry,'" I told him. "I feel like he's saying he should have taken better care of his health."

Then Ken asked, "Can you see him?"

"I don't think he was that tall," I said. "Was he under six feet?" Ken confirmed that he was. "He had dark hair?" Ken said yes. "At one point, did he have a mustache?" Again Ken said yes. "There's something funny about the mustache—he thinks he looks silly with it. He's joking about the mustache." Ken let out a laugh.

"I feel like your father was trying to build something while he was here," I said. "I don't mean like trying to build a house, but trying to build something on his own . . . and it was cut short. It was left incomplete. He wasn't so happy about that. When he crossed, his reaction was, 'Hey, wait a minute. You're kidding me. First of all, the Other Side is real? Secondly, I'm not going to be able to finish that?' He was annoyed about that."

Ken understood what this meant. His father was an artist who died in the middle of creating several pieces.

"Your father says he helps you with your work from the Other Side," I said. "Somehow he organizes things on the Other Side, and that helps your work here."

"So my father is helping me?"

"He's helping you now, and he's helped you for many years," I said. "Because he couldn't do it here physically, he's had to do it from the Other Side."

"I've always felt that," Ken said. Then he went on, "You might not be able to answer this, but I am curious. I'd like to know that in the event of my death, will I see my father?"

On the Other Side, I heard laughter.

"Well, absolutely!" I said. "Your father is laughing at you! He is saying, 'You're asking a question you already know the answer to!' Your father is joking with you and laughing and saying, 'First, there's going to be a tunnel and a great light, and then, if you like, I'll greet you first, and then you're going to see all of us there.' You have to believe that all your loved ones are going to greet you. And your father will be first in line."

———

The reality of an afterlife, the continuing presence of our loved ones who have crossed, the power of our connection to the Other Side, the brilliance of the light between us—for Ken, these aren't just data from a study. They are gifts to us from the Other Side.

And in our reading, they were a gift to him from his father.

"There is more waiting for us when we die, and we will be loved," Ken said in a recent conversation. "What we encounter will be beautiful, more beautiful than words can express. Because the truth is, we are connected to another world."

But even given his work in the field, despite all the research he's done, he realizes that, in the end, "we all have to solve the riddle of an afterlife for ourselves. And for me, I believe there is a beautiful afterlife. I believe we are never alone."

25

The Principal

SOMETIMES EVEN TEACHERS dread the walk to the principal's office.

I'd been teaching at Herricks High School for sixteen years and, except for one colleague—the one whom I'd seen would find a new car and girlfriend—and my closest friend, Stephanie—a fellow Herricks High School English teacher whom I'd confided in—no one knew about my abilities as a psychic medium. I'd worked hard to keep it a secret and make sure my two paths didn't cross . . . until one day they did.

A fellow teacher, one whose energy I really liked, named Suzanne, approached me after class.

"I went to a spiritual development seminar over the weekend," she said, "and the name Laura Lynne Jackson came up."

I felt my stomach seize. Suzanne explained she'd attended a lecture by Pat Longo, a well-known spiritual teacher and healer, in which she mentioned a reading she'd had with me.

"Is that you?" she asked me. "Are you that Laura Lynne Jackson?"

I nodded, though inside I felt a little panicky.

"Don't worry," Suzanne said with a smile, "your secret's safe with me."

A short time later I agreed to take part in a Forever Family Foundation event at a college on Long Island. The event was for people who had lost loved ones. I felt reasonably confident no one from my high school would know about it. I was wrong.

"I want to give you a heads-up," Suzanne wrote me in an email. "Danielle [another teacher in Suzanne's department] bought tickets to the event and she's organizing an outing with some other teachers. We're all going to be there."

When I told Garrett what was happening, he didn't hesitate.

"You have to tell the principal what you do," he said.

Garrett was right. I needed to know if my participation in the event would jeopardize my teaching career. If the principal told me I couldn't do it, I'd have to cancel—and that would crush me. I knew I'd be able to help a lot of people who were really suffering, and maybe I'd even be able to change some of their lives. But if it meant losing my job, I just couldn't do it.

And so I took the long, lonely walk to the principal's office.

Jane, who'd been the principal of Herricks High School for several years, was an education lifer. Raised on Long Island by an Irish mother and Greek father, she started out as a special education teacher and spent the next forty years in the system. At our high school she was responsible for more than thirteen hundred children from a wide range of backgrounds. On top of that, Jane somehow found time to teach a night class for teachers who wanted to become administrators. She was a passionate, hands-on educator, a beautiful person with a giving soul. I admired and respected her greatly, and in our eleven years together we'd gotten along very well.

Still, as I approached her office I was so nervous—just like a student who'd been sent to the principal.

I took a deep breath, went inside, and sat in the chair across from her desk.

"I need to tell you something," I began, trying to stop my hands from trembling. "I . . . I have this whole other life outside of school that no one knows about."

Jane looked concerned. I later learned that her first thought was, *Laura's a prostitute?*

"I'm not an overly religious person, but I am spiritual," I went on, grasping for the right words. "And there's this volunteer work I sometimes do on the weekends, and I'm going to be part of an event next month, and I want to make sure you're okay with it, and the administration is okay with it. And this volunteer work . . . the kind of work I do is . . . it involves me helping people understand about their loved ones. Loved ones who have crossed."

Jane looked at me intently.

"So," she said, "you're . . . sensitive?"

I nodded.

"You're . . . one of those?"

"Yes," I said.

"A medium?"

"Yes. A psychic medium."

Jane kept her eyes fixed on mine. I tried not to squirm or look away. The cat was all the way out of the bag now.

Then Jane leaned across the desk and in a whisper asked, "Laura, do you see anyone around me now?"

And just like that, the gates flew open. It was as if the Other Side had it planned all along. The Other Side came through a mile a minute. I hadn't been expecting to read Jane—I didn't want to read her. But someone on the Other Side was pushing hard, and Jane's question was all the opening that person needed. It was Jane's mother, who'd passed decades earlier.

"I'm hearing Margaret," I said. "Your mom is telling me the name Margaret."

Jane's mouth fell open. She got up, walked around her desk, and closed her office door. Then she sat back down and leaned in.

"Yes," she said. "Her name was Margaret."

"Your mother raised you very strictly," I went on. "She was a strict Catholic and she had all these rules for you, and she knows it was tough sometimes, but she wants you to know that everything she did was for you and your future, because she loves you very much."

Jane's eyes filled with tears.

Then I heard another word.

"Morphine. Your mom is saying something about morphine. She says you were always asking the doctors questions about morphine, and how much she should be given, and she wants to say thank you for being so involved, and so concerned, and for making the end of her life easier."

Jane had her face in her hands now. I kept going. There was something about Jane's son and his career in film, and about her daughter, and a baby I saw on the Other Side waiting to come to her daughter. The Other Side was filled with information for Jane. Before I knew it forty minutes had passed, and the class bell rang. Jane got up and came around her desk and hugged me.

"Your gift is beautiful," she said.

We agreed to talk again later. After sixth period, I saw Jane waiting for me outside my classroom.

"Can you come see me after ninth period?" she asked.

I felt like I'd been punched in the stomach. I feared that Jane had called the school district superintendent and that he had banned me from attending the event. I was anxious and distracted, but somehow made it through my last three classes. As I walked to Jane's office I felt the same dread as before.

When Jane's assistant saw me, her face turned red. Another secretary blushed and looked away. I realized Jane must have told them about me. Suddenly I looked different to them. They didn't know how to act around me.

Then Jane motioned me inside. She seemed solemn.

"I need to ask you something," she said softly.

I braced myself for bad news.

"It's about my husband," Jane said.

I felt the doors swing open again. I sat down across from Jane and let it all out.

"He is here," I said. "Your husband is here. He crossed a few years ago."

"Five years," Jane said.

"And you were married for a long time."

"Thirty-five years," she said.

"Your husband is here. And he wants you to know . . . that he loves what you are doing with the house."

Jane smiled and started to tear up again.

"But he is saying something about the birds," I continued. "The bird feeders. He says you haven't been filling the bird feeders like you should be. He wants you to fill them. He wants the birds to come back."

Jane wiped away tears. It was just a tiny detail, but to her it was personal and intimate, something the two of them had once shared, something that had been theirs alone. The bird feeders had been important to her husband—and it was true, she hadn't been keeping them filled. It was validation.

Her husband stayed with us for a long time. He offered several details about their life together, all to verify that he was there. After a while, Jane stopped me.

"Laura," she said, "can you ask him something for me? I need to know . . . How does he feel about . . . my husband now?"

I would later learn Jane was haunted by feelings of guilt for remarrying. She was such a strong, giving person, and she lived her life in such a proud and purposeful way, but she was also human, and all her strength couldn't push away the feeling that in remarrying she was betraying her first husband and the memory of their thirty-five years together. She was still mourning his loss, and her guilt became the burden she believed it was necessary to bear.

"How does he feel about my new husband?" she asked again, almost imploringly.

The answer came through clearly and strongly.

"Jane," I said, "he is the one who brought your new husband to you."

Jane looked stunned. Her first husband was insistent, so I kept talking.

"He says your husband now is a bit of a goofball, and he likes that about him. He likes his personality. But he says . . ."

I hesitated, surprised by what I was hearing.

"He says he's the one with the cuter butt."

Jane laughed.

"He says all he ever wanted for you was happiness. That's why he sent your new husband to you. He wants you to be happy. That hasn't changed. It will never change. Not even when you let him go, Jane. Especially not then."

It was not the conversation I'd expected to have with the principal. The next day, Jane pulled me aside again and asked me a straightforward question.

"What is your view of the world?"

My answer came easily.

"I see the earth as a classroom," I said. "We are all sent here to learn lessons and help each other. But the real world is the spirit world. And that world is a world of light and love."

Jane gave me her blessing to continue as both a teacher and a psychic medium. We worked out a protocol for what I'd tell the students if they ever found out, but otherwise I just went back to the business of being a teacher. Sometime that week Jane called the district superintendent and explained my situation. Thanks in part to her recommendation, the district signed off, and my job was safe. The superintendent's assistant even asked for a reading herself.

"Personally, I don't believe in that stuff," the superintendent told Jane.

"Neither did I," Jane said, "until now."

———

For sixteen years I'd lived in fear of my secret being exposed, all because I'd convinced myself that people wouldn't accept me for who I was. For some reason I believed that when my secret got out I'd be shunned, ridiculed, fired, or all three. I never imagined that the people around me might be supportive. So I let my decisions be governed by fear.

How counterproductive fear can be! How crippling and wasteful! I was even prepared to give up my work as a medium. And then, in the end, Jane was wonderfully supportive. She not only accepted my gift but embraced it. All that fear and dread and worry had unnecessarily shackled me for sixteen years.

I can't tell you how good it felt to finally be free of the fear.

My reading with Jane, she later told me, also had a profound effect on her life. Before that day, she didn't spend much time thinking about an afterlife. She considered herself a spiritual person, but she was also very pragmatic. She tried to be good and honest and loving, but she also accepted that her existence was finite. If there was something more beyond this life, then great. But she didn't dwell on it. She didn't find it relevant. She only tried to get the most out of her earthly life now.

But after our reading, Jane's view of the world changed.

"I was okay with just dying," she told me. "But now I am open to something truly wonderful happening afterward. And so my life has become about being in a state of readiness. It is about experiencing the connection we all have to this world of light and love, and living our very best lives now."

26

Touching the Cords

IN 2013 PHRAN AND BOB GINSBERG invited me to be a facilitating medium at the Forever Family Foundation's annual weekend retreat. The event was called "Transforming Grief: Connections and Healing Between Two Worlds," and it took place at a hotel and conference center in Chester, Connecticut. It was a beautiful setting, with acres of lush woodlands and a tree-shaded deck overlooking a lovely pond. Phran told me the event was designed "to deal with the challenges of loss and grief and to focus on ways we can all communicate with deceased loved ones and maintain our relationships with them."

I had just arrived and checked in to my room when my cellphone rang. When I answered, all I heard was silence, so I hung up. A few minutes later, it rang again. Again no one was there.

That night, I got six or seven more calls from nowhere. Around the fourth time I started to think something strange was happening. One dropped call, maybe two, no big deal. But six or seven?

Was I being pranked? The odd thing was that no phone number showed up on the caller ID. The phone just rang.

After a while, I realized what the calls were about: someone on the Other Side was trying to get through.

Phantom calls are one of the many ways those on the Other Side send us messages. Cellphones emit electromagnetic waves, which is a kind of energy the Other Side can manipulate. It also made sense that I got the phantom calls at an event that invites the Other Side in. At these retreats I've seen people whose anguish is coiled so tightly in their chests they can barely breathe. I've felt the weight of grief so heavy it feels like a cloud of lead. But I've also seen people find hope and meaning right before my eyes. I've watched tears of pure love where before there were tears of rage. I've seen people simply let go of their grief, like a child letting go of a balloon. And I have listened to what the Other Side tells us about loss and grief. The phantom calls, I was sure, held some lesson for me.

The first evening of the retreat, Bob and Phran welcomed all the participants and presented the weekend's agenda. I noticed a couple sitting perfectly still, keeping to themselves, their eyes cast down toward the floor. Their faces were like stone. I could feel the heaviness of their grief. Their pain was palpable. I said a silent prayer to the Other Side: *Please allow me to be a vehicle to help them.* I hoped that whoever it was that they had lost would find me.

That night, we gathered around a campfire outside. Phran had asked if I'd be "open" in case anyone's loved ones on the Other Side wanted to come through. "Of course," I told her. After everyone had settled around the fire, we sang songs to raise our energy. When the singing stopped, a hushed sadness settled back in. I felt the pull. It was time to do a reading.

I waited to be guided toward someone—to feel the energy lasso. Suddenly I felt a strong pull in the direction of the sad couple I'd noticed earlier. I made my way to them on the other side of the campfire. The pull got stronger. Whoever needed to communicate with them was being very insistent. I stood in front of them and let the visitor through.

"You've lost a son," I said.

===

Fred and Susan had been married for twenty years and raised three sons, Scott, Tyler, and Bobby. Their life in Thunder Bay, Ontario, would be familiar to many—a flurry of hockey practices, baseball games, school events, and homework assignments. All three boys were extremely bright and athletic, though Scott, the oldest, was the most outgoing, a natural leader. He was the kind of boy who'd suddenly start singing in the middle of a class, and before you knew it all the other students were singing along, too, and somehow that only endeared him to teachers more.

In high school Scotty was voted student council president and junior prom king. He played several sports and excelled at them. He also was certified as a scuba diver. He was accepted into the prestigious Canadian Memorial Chiropractic College.

Toward the end of his first semester, he returned home during a break to study for his exams. "Every day he sat at the dining table with his books open. He pored over them," Susan later told me. "He didn't go out, he just studied. Except for that one Friday night."

That Friday night, Scotty and his friend Ethan went to a party, after which Scotty slept over at Ethan's house. The next day, around 1:00 p.m., Susan and Fred were out shopping—they were planning a big Easter dinner for the family—when Susan got a call from Ethan's brother.

"Scotty fell down some stairs last night," he told her. "He was disoriented, so we called an ambulance. He is on his way to the hospital."

She and Fred drove straight to the hospital and went to the ER. A doctor told them they couldn't see Scotty yet. There had been some trauma, but no one knew how much.

"We are going to put him under general anesthesia," the doctor said, "and then we're going to call the neurosurgeon."

The neurosurgeon? Susan thought. Didn't he just tumble down some stairs? She heard the doctor page the neurosurgeon, and she froze with fear.

They waited in a private room with Ethan and his brother. Susan and Fred paced in and out of the room, anxiously looking down the hallway where their son was being treated. After what felt like an eternity, the doctor came to see them.

"She went right to Fred and talked directly to him," Susan says. "She didn't even look at me. That's when I knew it was bad."

There was severe swelling in Scotty's brain. He remained under sedation. The neurosurgeon tried to insert a tube to relieve the pressure, but there was too much swelling. Then doctors tried to increase Scotty's blood pressure to force his body to redistribute the blood, and his heart rate was elevated to an unnatural 250 beats a minute, but this too failed to reduce the swelling.

The only remaining option for doctors was to drill through Scotty's skull to alleviate the pressure on his brain. One of the doctors who assisted in the surgery was a friend, and after it was over he found Fred and Susan in the waiting room.

"When we went in we found so much swelling on his brain," the surgeon explained. "There was nothing we could do."

Scotty hadn't died. But he couldn't breathe on his own, and the pressure on his brain had done considerable damage.

"If it was my son," the doctor said, "I would let him go. He'll never be Scotty again."

Just like that. Not just sudden, but unthinkable. Not possible. Susan and Fred, in shock, called Tyler and Bobby to the hospital and met with the surgeon. They knew what was coming, but they wanted to face it together.

"The truth is, Scotty isn't with us anymore," the surgeon said.

The family had to decide whether or not to take Scotty off life support. Earlier that year, when Scotty had gotten his driver's license, he'd enthusiastically agreed to be an organ donor. The doctors explained that because Scotty was so young and fit, they had a chance to harvest some of his organs, but the decision had to be made right away. Susan asked, "How do you know Scotty won't get better? How do you know for sure?"

The doctor went through the list of criteria they use to determine such things: not being able to breathe on your own, extreme damage to the brain stem, unresponsiveness to pain, no reflexes. There was no doubt: Scotty was gone.

The family took a few moments to process what they'd heard. In their hearts, they knew what they had to do, but it was nevertheless an unfathomably difficult decision.

They told the doctor to remove Scotty from life support.

On Wednesday, April 4, 2012, a team of doctors wheeled Scotty toward an operating room to harvest his organs. The family accompanied them partway but could not go beyond the doors of the operating room. At the entrance to the operating room the doctors stepped away from the gurney, and Scotty's parents and brothers, one by one, laid their hands on Scotty's body to say goodbye.

"Goodbye, my son," his father said through tears.

"Goodbye, Scott," his mother said. "We will love you forever."

The doctors pushed the gurney through the doors of the operating room, and Scotty's family stood there as the doors swung closed.

Within hours several helicopters landed at the hospital to pick up Scotty's organs. His lungs, his liver, his pancreas, and his kidneys all went to different places, to different recipients. The last organ to be harvested was Scotty's heart. The final helicopter surged into the sky and took Scotty's heart away.

Back at home, Scotty's medical books still lay open on the dining room table.

At the retreat I read for Fred and Susan for forty minutes. The young man who came through was vibrant and determined and had a lot to say. He gave me an *S* for his name and told me he had crossed quickly. It had been an accident, he said, and he took some responsibility for it. Then he provided a series of validations, as if he understood his parents would need to be persuaded he was there.

"He is showing me something green," I told them. "A green costume. He is telling me to mention it to his mother, because his mother will laugh."

At first, Susan looked shocked. Then, just as predicted, she laughed. "Scotty dressed up head to toe as the Hulk on Halloween," Susan later explained. "I laughed because it was just like Scotty to bring that up to try to make me laugh."

Next, Scotty told me to bring up the earrings his mother was wearing. I asked Susan if she'd been undecided about which earrings to wear that day.

"Scotty is saying that he likes the pair you are wearing, and he encouraged you to pick that pair over the other one you were thinking about," I said. Susan confirmed that she'd settled on a pair but at the last moment went back and switched to the pair she was wearing. This was Scotty's way of showing his mother he'd been with her all day.

Then I turned to Fred. "Okay, this is a little embarrassing, but I always have to pass along any messages I get," I told him. "Scotty wants me to tell you he likes your new underwear. It's a new style, he's saying. No more tighty-whities."

Now it was Fred's turn to be stunned. "Scotty always teased me about my old Jockey-style shorts," Fred explained later. "Then just a few days earlier I bought brand-new underwear that was more like boxers. No one knew I did that."

I continued, "He also says to tease you about your shoes, but he's laughing because he says you now have enough shoes to last you ten years." Susan and Fred looked at each other and laughed. "It's true," Fred said. "There's this one style of shoe I really like. Look—I have them on now. And they went on sale, so I figured, 'Why not?' and I ordered a whole bunch from the website."

Scotty then showed me a garden, and I felt an overwhelming sense of love.

"Scotty is showing me a garden connected to him and to both of you," I said. "He says you sit by it and he is saying he sits there with you. It is very beautiful. It's beautiful that you spend time there, connecting with him. It's a quiet place for you to do that."

"We planted a garden in his memory," Susan said. "We call it Scotty's garden. It's so special to us."

"You don't need me to see and feel and hear Scotty," I told them. "You are already doing it. You do it when you sit with him in his garden. And you do it when you are shopping for underwear and picking out earrings. He is with you always. He is still part of the family."

Susan and Fred had been so deeply entrenched in their grief when they first arrived that I'd worried they wouldn't be able to find a way through it. But in the end Scotty took care of all that. When he came through he was so much fun. He had us all laughing and smiling! He came through as the Scotty his family loved so much.

But the most important thing Scotty shared was his excitement.

"He is saying he is just so thrilled, because what you're doing in his name enables him to continue to make a difference here on earth," I told them. "He is so thankful that he can still have an impact here even though he's on the Other Side. He is surprised and thrilled by it. All of you are working together as a team of light to help others—the two of you here, and Scotty on the Other Side. And that just makes him so happy."

I didn't know what Scotty was referring to at the time, but later I learned that in the year after he passed, his parents arranged an annual memorial dinner to raise funds for charities in Scott's name. They scheduled the event for the Saturday closest to his birthday in November. The first dinner, held at a popular restaurant in Thunder Bay, drew more than a hundred people and raised $36,000 for a charity that helps feed children in West Africa. Since then they have raised thousands of dollars for a group called Kids in Syria and more than $50,000 for hungry children in Mali.

"We call it Scotty's Dinner," Susan told me. "Scotty really loved children and he loved helping children. I have young people coming to me all the time to tell me what a difference Scotty made in their lives."

Scotty needed his parents to know how thankful he was for what they were doing in his name.

He had one more message for them before we were done.

"He is thanking you for coming to this grief retreat," I said. "He is saying he was trying to get you here, and then you almost didn't come. He was so happy that you decided to come. He doesn't want you to deal with your grief alone."

There is a reason I gladly participate in grief retreats. I go in seeing how distraught people are, and I leave seeing how their burdens have been lifted by the act of sharing their grief with others.

By sharing, we are acknowledging that, as spiritual beings, we are all connected.

Grief brings us great pain, but the Other Side teaches us that this pain is not about the absence of love—it's about the continuation of that love. The brilliant cords of love that connect us to someone in this life endure into the afterlife. And when we feel unbearable pain at the loss of a loved one, it is like we are tugging on that cord of love. The pain is real because the cord is real. Our love doesn't end—it goes on.

Finally, Fred and Susan's reading showed me yet again that what we do on this earth in the wake of losing a loved one matters greatly.

The most powerful way we can honor someone who has crossed is to spread light and love in their name. Doing that work not only keeps that person present in our lives but also allows our loved one on the Other Side to still be a positive influence on our world.

It all matters! If we run a 5K race in someone's honor, that person will be running or walking with us. If we hold a charity dinner, that person will be at our table. Our loved ones on the Other Side always know what we are doing, and when they see us spreading light in their names, it matters greatly to them. The Other Side wants us to live wide-open, vibrant lives. Live as fully and brightly as we can. They will be there with us.

When we turn tragedy into hope, our loved ones on the Other Side don't just see this, they celebrate it.

That night after I read for Susan and Fred, I received even more phantom calls on my cellphone. But this time I had an idea of who was pranking me. I found Fred and Susan at breakfast the next morning and told them about the phantom calls. "I feel they were from Scotty," I said. "I feel he wants me to tell you he is still around and talking to you. And that you don't need me in order to feel that connection. I think he's having a bit of fun and showing off what he can do."

I would later learn that the calls from nowhere weren't Scotty's only attempts to keep the pathways between him and his parents open. Scotty, it turns out, has a fondness for expressing himself through electricity. "When he was young he was fascinated by electricity," Susan says, "so I'm not surprised that he still is."

Susan even had her own weird cellphone experience. "We were down in Florida, and I saw there was a message on my phone," she says. "I played it back, but it was blank. I said, 'Scotty, if that's you, you have to do better than one blank message.'" Later that day, Susan found ninety-five blank messages on her cell.

Going forward, Fred and Susan will continue the Scotty Dinners, and they will look for new ways to honor their ongoing connection to their son.

"We feel it is our role to keep Scott's light alive in this world by doing good things in his name," says Susan. "It's a way he can continue to have a positive influence on people. He can still make a difference in this world."

"It doesn't mean we don't still miss him each and every day," says Fred. "It doesn't make the grief go away. But it makes it easier knowing that Scotty is always right by our side, still a part of our team."

27

The Phoenix

AT THE SAME GRIEF RETREAT where I met Scotty's parents I did a series of group readings for ten to twelve participants at a time. On the last day of the retreat, as I began my fourth and final session, I felt the energy lasso guide me to a man and woman sitting together. As I approached them, an image appeared—a dark, disturbing image. Then more images, all of them gruesome. I saw images of impact and destruction. I saw flames and smoke.

"Someone is coming through for you," I told the man. "She is saying she died in a car crash."

The man looked up at me, tears filling his eyes.

One night in 1966 Frank McGonagle and his wife, Charlotte, got into his Triumph TR4 sports car to drive from Boston to Swansea, Massachusetts, an hour south. They had just attended a wake for

Frank's uncle, and they were anxious to get home to their four young children. With just a few miles to go, on a quiet highway, Frank drove up to an intersection and stopped as the light turned from yellow to red.

In the next moment a car roared up behind them and hit the back of the TR4. The impact was devastating. The car was slammed into the intersection and sent crashing into a guardrail. The smell of gasoline filled the air. Three teenage boys jumped out of another car and rushed to the Triumph. They reached through the shattered driver's-side window and pulled Frank out. Just as they did, the gas tank exploded.

Flames engulfed the car. Frank, too, was on fire. He dropped and rolled, trying to stop the burning. He was wearing an overcoat, which protected most of his body. But his head was exposed, and he suffered third-degree burns on his face, ears, scalp, and neck. Frank doesn't remember being pulled out of the car or rolling on the highway. In fact, he can barely remember the crash at all. He remembers waking up in the ER, and a doctor telling him his wife didn't make it.

Charlotte, the beautiful, curly-haired Texas girl he'd fallen for the day he met her—the love of his life, the mother of his children, his everything—was gone. Charlotte had been seven months pregnant. In the blink of an eye, the life they had built disappeared.

———

In my reading with Frank, the Other Side didn't tell me all the details about his life after the crash, but I did see it had been difficult. The truth is, when Frank woke up in the emergency room, he woke up in a kind of hell.

He was shot full of morphine, with a tracheostomy tube in his neck. "Right from that moment, I felt I was responsible for her death," Frank told me. "I felt I had abandoned ship. I could not forgive myself for leaving her."

Frank spent the next three months in the hospital. His burns were life-threatening, but he pulled through. Worse than the physical damage, though, was the guilt and the sense of unfairness, which nearly crippled him. While he was still in the hospital, a priest came to visit him. The priest knew the driver of the car that had caused the accident, a young man named Richard, who wanted to meet Frank.

"He wants to ask your forgiveness," the priest said.

"Father, if you bring him into this room," Frank said, "I will kill him."

Friends and family helped Frank recover and raise his four young children. But trying to keep his family together without Charlotte was almost unbearable. At times Frank contemplated suicide. About eighteen months after the accident he married a nurse who worked at the hospital where he'd been treated, but the marriage was doomed from the start. "I was a mess," Frank explained. "I hadn't resolved any of my issues of guilt and rage and grief."

Ten years passed, then twenty, then thirty, and Frank was still struggling.

Then he attended a speech by Fred Luskin, a Ph.D. who was addressing a room of burn victims. Luskin talked about the power of forgiveness, about how forgiveness helps the one who is forgiven but also the one who forgives. Luskin made a persuasive case for the way in which forgiveness could change the dynamics of a tragedy. "I had to meet Richard," Frank later told me. "And I had to forgive him."

Richard, Frank learned, had eventually been convicted of reckless endangerment. He'd paid a fine and lost his license for a year. "One day I spoke with a neighbor who knew Richard," Frank said. "He told me Richard had never driven again after the crash."

The neighbor helped arrange a meeting between Frank and Richard in the rectory of a local church. Frank arrived first, too nervous to sit. He looked out the rectory window and watched a car pull up. A man stepped out of the passenger side and walked haltingly toward the entrance. Frank drew a deep breath. He heard footsteps and watched as the rectory door slowly opened.

At last the two men were in the same room, just a few feet apart. For a long time, neither said a word. Frank wrestled with a flood of emotions.

Finally Frank spoke.

"Thank you for coming," he said. "I know it took a lot of courage to be here."

Richard looked up. His eyes were red and he was shaking.

"I am sorry," he said. "I am so, so sorry."

"Look," Frank went on, "I know you didn't intend for this to happen, but it happened. At times I've driven irresponsibly myself. In the end, I know you didn't mean to do it."

The two men spoke for half an hour. Frank realized Richard had been punishing himself more harshly than anyone else could have.

At last the men wiped away their tears, shook hands, and said goodbye. Richard left, and Frank watched him walk to the curb and wait for his ride. Finally a car pulled up and Richard climbed in. Frank realized he wasn't the only one lost in a world of grief.

Two days later, Frank was on the phone with his daughter, Margaret. He told her about his meeting with Richard and how he had forgiven him. And as he spoke, a simple question formed in his head.

Now that you've forgiven him, why don't you forgive yourself?

After that, Frank's perspective changed dramatically. "I was able to be more objective about what happened," he says. "It was like a dispatch of ego. I became more of an observer than a participant. The meeting with Richard is what started it. As I watched him walk away I felt so sorry for him. I felt such a deep sense of pity. I could see how hurt and wounded he was, and how he will probably always be. That was a complete reversal of how I felt after the crash happened, when I probably would have killed him. I was starting to see the power of forgiveness."

Slowly Frank began letting go of his guilt. And when he did, he experienced the power of forgiveness to heal.

But letting go of his grief was another matter. There was one profound question he simply couldn't answer: what had become of Charlotte? One minute she'd been with him, and the next she was gone. Where had she gone? What had happened to her? As far as Frank was concerned, his relationship with Charlotte ended abruptly on that long-ago day and the powerful love between them was simply extinguished.

Frank thought back to the day Charlotte's mother and father had come to see him in the hospital after the crash. He was dreading the moment. Charlotte had been their only child, a brilliant, beautiful sun goddess. But when Charlotte's mother walked into his room, she sat in a chair beside Frank's bed and said, "Frank, Charlotte is still with you. Charlotte came to me in the bedroom, and she wants you to know she is okay. She is not in pain. She is in heaven with your baby, and she is very happy. And she wants you to get well and be a strong father for your four children. She wants you to be happy."

Through the haze of his morphine, only one thing went through Frank's mind as he listened to Charlotte's mother. *She's talking mumbo jumbo,* he thought. *She is deranged with grief.*

It would take more than forty years for that to change.

———

In 2006, a friend urged Frank to attend a seminar led by a psychic medium. The friend thought it might help Frank in his journey. Frank was skeptical, but he agreed to go. During the seminar, he listened as several psychics summoned details about his deceased relatives. One of the psychics even held up a sign that said CC—the initials of his late wife, Charlotte, whose maiden name was Carlisle. That was enough for Frank to change his thinking about the Other Side. He now believed it was possible for him to somehow connect with Charlotte again.

During my reading with Frank, Charlotte came through more clearly than she had in any of Frank's previous readings. She showed me how, in the years that followed, she watched over Frank and steered him to his current wife, Arlene, who was the woman beside him at the retreat. "She wants to thank Arlene for everything she has done for you," I told Frank. "She says you have a lot of people, a lot of guides and loved ones, who are looking out for you on the Other Side."

Charlotte communicated a deep sense of pride for what her husband had done since the crash. It seemed there was a whole team of people on the Other Side praising and celebrating Frank.

"They are saying you deserve a standing ovation for the work you've done on this earth," I said.

I later learned Frank had spent thirty years helping other burn victims cope with their injuries and find ways to lead normal lives. He began working with a national support organization called the Phoenix Society for Burn Survivors, and he went on to become president of the group's board. "I truly believe that is one of the main reasons I was spared," Frank wrote in one newsletter. "I survived to help other burn survivors and their families. It is not my obligation. It is my privilege."

Now Charlotte was coming through to express how proud she was of her husband for what he had accomplished. It was a cascade of joy and affection—a pure expression of love. "Charlotte sees how much you have given back to the world, and how you didn't allow what happened to make you bitter," I told him. "She wants to acknowledge everything you've done in her honor."

Frank began to well up. He believed Charlotte had watched out for him and been part of his journey all along. He believed she'd steered him to Arlene. And he believed she'd seen him help hundreds of other survivors, all in her memory.

"Everything I did, I did to honor Charlotte," Frank later told me. "It was a way of making it so that she wasn't completely gone. To learn that she was proud of me, that she was happy with what I was doing, well, that was incredibly comforting."

And yet Charlotte wasn't the only one who came through during the reading.

"Frank, I see a spirit who was not born," I told him. "The spirit died in the crash, too. Frank, it is your son."

Frank looked at me in disbelief.

"Your son is coming through and he wants me to acknowledge that he is also so happy to see that you are helping other people," I told him. "Your son is very, very proud of you."

When the crash happened, Frank and Charlotte had yet to choose a name for their unborn child. Over the years, whenever he thought about the child he'd lost, he thought about him only as "baby boy."

And now, at the grief retreat, his baby boy was a baby no more—he was a beautiful spirit of light and love. He hadn't been able to reach Frank on this earth, but he was reaching him now, expressing love and pride.

Frank put his face in his hands and wept.

For decades, Frank had kept some boxes of Super 8 film reels stored in a closet of his home. They were old home movies, with scratchy, shaky, silent, bleached-color images of Frank, Charlotte, and their young children. To Frank, they were reminders of a life that had been taken away. He could not bear to watch them again after Charlotte died. But after our reading, Frank took out the boxes.

"There was about two hours of film," he later told me. "It covered the births of all our kids and went right up to the time of the crash. I converted it all to digital and cut it together. I wanted to do it for my kids. I wanted to do it for Charlotte."

The short movie tells the story of a beautiful, happy family. Charlotte smiles and waves at the camera. The children toddle around and fall. There is joy and laughter and love—lots of love. Frank gave the movie to his children so that they could remember Charlotte the way he remembered her. Frank also wanted his eleven grandchildren to watch the movie so that they could know who their grandmother had been. "It was another way to honor Charlotte," Frank said.

When the retreat was over, I went back home to Long Island and thought a lot about Frank's story. What made it so incredibly moving to me was how he had been able to find the strength and courage to turn the darkness in his life into a bright, beautiful light. Frank's story, I realized, could teach us how to shift our perspective of what grief means.

In certain cultures there is a tradition of soldiering on alone through tragedy—as if "keeping a stiff upper lip" is a quality to be admired above all else. But grief research shows that walling ourselves away from others in times of grief is in fact detrimental to healing.

Early on, Frank suffered through his sadness alone. Eventually he gravitated to burn survivor support groups, and that's when his healing truly began. "Men are taught to be John Wayne," Frank said. "We're taught not to cry or share our pain. But when I began to share my story with other survivors, I could see how much that helped." When he forgave the man who caused the crash, he was able to turn the act of forgiving to himself, and that allowed him to make himself available to others.

The universe is designed for us to be there for each other—we are not meant to retreat into our pain and grief alone. We are meant to honor the vibrant cords of light and love that bind us, because the love of others is the most healing force of all. Why would we shut ourselves off from this powerful force? We are meant to be part of a vast, endless cycle of love, through which we receive the love of others and then pass that love on to someone else.

Sharing our pain, and giving and receiving love, is how we heal our grief.

Today, every morning when he gets up, Frank goes into the shower and says thanks. "I have a long list of people I talk to," he told me. "I talk to Charlotte every day and I ask her to keep on helping me. I talk to all the loved ones I've lost, all my spirits and guides. I know a lot of people would be skeptical about that, but I have changed my belief in how the universe works."

And even on the days when he still grieves for and misses Charlotte, he comforts himself with the knowledge that she isn't really gone. "I believe Charlotte is still with me," he says. "I believe my baby boy is with me. I believe all my loved ones are here, giving me love. What I've figured out is that it all has to do with love. When you love someone, you love them forever."

28

The Bonsai Tree

IN THE COURSE of my readings, the Other Side helped me answer many of the big questions I'd long grappled with.

Why are we here? To learn. To give and receive love. To be the agents of positive change in the world.

What happens when we die? We shed our bodies but our consciousness endures.

What is our true purpose on this earth? To grow in love—and to help others do the same.

The Other Side has also helped me answer a question that still confounds many thinkers: Do we have free will to chart the course of our lives, or are our futures already mapped out? The Other Side has shown me a model of existence that is generous enough to encompass both free will—the ability to act at one's own discretion—and predeterminism, which is the belief that all events and actions are decided in advance. It is a beautifully simple model I call "free will vs. points of fate."

Our existence is mapped out by a dazzling array of destination points that are in place before we are born. These are the points of fate—a continuum of all the crucial events, decisive moments, and significant people that constitute our time here. Think of them as stars in the night sky, a collection of beacons spread across a broad canvas.

The Other Side has shown me that we create the actions that move us from one point of fate to the next. We are the ones who connect the dots. We make the decisions that move us from one point to another, and in the process we shape and create the picture of our lives.

Each one of us comes into this life with unique gifts and unique contributions to make. Finding and honoring our true selves will always help us navigate our points of fate.

We must learn to recognize our own light. We must always let our truths and gifts and light guide our paths.

There are no "right" or "wrong" paths—just different lessons we learn on different paths. There are, however, definitely higher and lower paths, and taking the higher one can make learning our lessons easier. If we honor our own truths, our unique gifts, and our own light, we create a very beautiful picture indeed. And if we consistently do this, we find ourselves on our true path.

While we are choosing which path to take, our loved ones on the Other Side are hoping that we will make the best choice—and even at times exerting pull to help us find it. They want us to be the best versions of ourselves and achieve happiness and fulfillment.

Ultimately, though, it is up to us to make the choices, and that is where free will comes in. Sometimes we make decisions that lead us down a path of fear rather than a path of love. When that happens, we can veer off course and become lost.

But we must never forget that we all have the innate capacity to honor the pull and get back on the true path.

=====

During a reading for a woman named Nicole, whom I knew from the high school where I taught, a very strong presence emerged with urgent messages for her father, Mike. I explored some of those messages with Nicole, but it was clear to me that the Other Side wanted to get through to Mike. I asked Nicole to pass on the messages to her father, and a few months later Mike contacted me for a reading.

I typically don't know anything about a sitter, but with Mike a few facts came up in my reading with his daughter. I knew that he had two grown children and that he lived in Los Angeles and wrote screenplays. I also had a sense of what the Other Side was trying to convey to him. Still, I needed the Other Side to come through again to make sense of it all.

I began by reading Mike's energy. The left-hand side of my screen was flooded with bright orange. "Orange has to do with creativity and art," I explained. "Your energy marks you as an artist. Your guides are telling me that at age seven you knew you were an artist. You knew that was what you wanted to do.

"But I'm also seeing that around the age of eleven, that got shut down. For most of your life, you didn't honor the essence of who you are. Your life has been a battle to embrace your passions and to love yourself, and most of your life you've been confused and searching for answers from the inside out."

"Yes," Mike said softly. "That's all true."

"I can see that your childhood was difficult," I went on. "Your father struggled with a lot of issues, and he was stunted and never got past those issues. A great portion of your struggle has been finding your voice and shaking off all the things your father imposed on you. Your father was a very forceful energy in your childhood."

Mike sighed and said, "Yes, he was."

People on the Other Side were pushing hard to get through, so I let them in.

"I see Mom and Dad on the Other Side," I told Mike. "But your father is pulling away and holding back. He is standing way behind your mom. So it will be your mom who talks first."

Mike's mother began by creating an absolute shower of love. Sometimes I will be overwhelmed by the force and sweep of someone's love, and this was one of those times.

"Mike," I said, "your mother is saying, 'I did not choose to leave you.' You need to know this. She says she would never have chosen to leave you."

Mike later explained that his mother died during open-heart surgery when he was nineteen. But because her marriage to his father was so difficult, Mike had believed that, in a way, his mother simply gave up on living. As a result, Mike spent much of his life feeling abandoned.

In the reading Mike's mother was insistent. "She says she is sorry for not protecting you more from your father, but she needs you to know that she would never have chosen to go. She did not want to leave her children alone with your father."

At that moment, Mike interrupted the reading to tell me a story about the day his mother died.

His father had called him to tell him she was ill, but that was all he knew. So Mike got in his 1957 Thunderbird and drove home from Boston, four hours away. "And as I was driving, a white flash of light came into the car," Mike said. "And I knew it was her, and I could feel her relief, and so I felt relieved, too. I felt elation. She came to me to tell me she was all right. That she had been released from a bad marriage and a crippled body, the result of a stroke years earlier. The happy, buoyant feeling of her release stayed with me for the rest of the long ride home. I knew in my heart she was finally at peace."

At the precise moment Mike's mother came to him in his car, the clock on his dashboard froze. "It never worked again," Mike said.

When Mike got home, he found his father in tears. It was the first time he'd ever seen him cry.

"Your mother is dead," he said.

But Mike already knew. "Yes," he said, and without another word he went to his room.

Mike's relationship with his father, Mario, had been defined by a lack of affection and a failure to connect. At six foot two and more than 250 pounds, Mario was a physically commanding presence. He was a firm believer that men should never show their emotions.

Mike knew he couldn't share what he had experienced in his car with his father, so he didn't even try. In fact, Mike never told anyone about the experience.

The significance of that moment—the missed opportunity for Mike and his father to share something important—filled me with sadness. "Mike, there is a brick wall between you and your father," I said. "Everyone in your family was an island unto themselves. For most of your life you've been fragmented—you've been torn between being yourself and being the version of you that your father demanded."

The urgency of the Other Side to get through to Mike was starting to make sense. He'd been badly damaged by something that happened to him in his childhood—something to do with his father. Decades later, he was still grappling with these very issues. It was as if the universe had stolen something from him when he was a kid, and now it wanted to give it back.

And that is the moment when Mike's father finally came through.

He came through meekly, at first, with his head down trying to get out an apology.

"It starts when you were three," I told Mike. "Did . . . did your father hit you when you were three? He is showing me in shame that he hit you. And you were so tiny."

"If I did something bad, he would chase me around the neighborhood," Mike said. "I'd run home and hide in the closet, and he would find me and hit me."

"Mike, your father is bowing his head and shuffling his feet and muttering an apology," I told him. "He has been made to see what he did, and he apologizes to you. He started beating you when you were three, and it is hurting me to see this, and I need to tell you that you didn't do anything wrong. You were just a helpless, innocent boy. It was all in your dad's head. And you need to know this, because you still struggle with it.

"You were like a child who was held underwater until he almost drowned. Finally your father left and you came up and you could barely breathe, and today you are still gasping for air. But you need to know it was not your fault. Your dad is taking responsibility for what happened."

Then Mario showed me a timeline with an event marked when Mike was nine. There was another mark at age eleven. I couldn't make out what these events were, but I could tell they had knocked Mike off his course.

"You chose a path for yourself that was not authentic," I told him. "Instead, you followed the model your dad imposed on you. And now your father—your father is weeping on the Other Side. He says what he did to you was unforgivable, and he is crying with shame. He is so ashamed and so sad and so sorry for what he did."

I could not see exactly what happened to Mike when he was nine and eleven. His father wasn't clear about it; he was too overwhelmed by remorse.

But then Mike started talking. He took me back to his childhood on Long Island. He had a collection of stuffed animals he loved dearly. A little yellow monkey with a long tail, a small brown bear, eight or nine animals in all. "They were my best friends," Mike said. "Growing up, there was no hugging or kissing in my house, but with my animals I could hug and kiss them all I wanted. I could relate to them. So I bunched them up beside me in bed and wrapped my arms around them every night."

One day when he was nine, Mike came home from school to find all the animals gone. He searched for them frantically, but they were nowhere to be found. His father had put them in the trash. "My dad said only sissies play with stuffed animals, so he threw them out," Mike said.

Two years later, when he was eleven, Mike found a large cardboard box outside a neighbor's home and pulled it into his family's garage. He cut it open and laid it flat and turned it into a giant canvas. Every day he would race home from school to work on his painting. It was a landscape with mountains and trees and streams. It was his masterpiece. Working on the painting made him feel alive. In that painting, Mike could see a reflection of his own beautiful light. He saw and understood his unique gifts and his true self.

One afternoon Mike came home from school, pulled up the garage door, and saw that his painting was gone. He asked his mother what had happened.

"Your father threw it away," she told him.

Mike didn't have to ask why. He already knew. He'd heard his father say it often enough: only sissies paint.

"To this day, I can still remember the shock of pulling up the garage door and not seeing my painting," Mike told me. "After that, I never painted again. I shut down my artistic side completely."

Instead, Mike chose a more practical path that led him to become a sales manager for Johnson & Johnson. It was a good job, but to Mike that's all it was—a job. Once in a while, when he got older, he'd try to paint again, but he never really pursued it. Or he'd think about writing something, but then drop it. He just didn't believe in himself anymore.

Mike's impulse to create something—and the gifts and abilities that comprised the very core of his being—lay dormant for decades.

—————

The universe, though, doesn't want to see us bury our dreams beneath layers of pain and doubt. Mike told me that several years ago, after he went through a divorce, he found himself in a group therapy session. A friend had insisted he go. A few weeks into the session, the therapist asked the people in the group to offer their thoughts about each other. All nine told Mike they thought he was a jerk.

"I was shocked," he said. "I didn't realize that's how people saw me. I still didn't know how to express emotion, so I was very dismissive of people, waving them off with my hand or using a bad tone of voice. As I drove myself home that night, I thought, *Well, here's a bunch of sensitive people all saying the same thing. I guess I've got to take a look at this.*"

That might have been the first moment of serious introspection in Mike's life.

After that, his life began to change. He'd never had female friends, but now he began to reach out to women as friends, and he found that with them he could express himself in ways that were impossible before. "I got to have conversations I could never have with men," he said. "That's when the door cracked wide open for me."

Mike had always felt a pull to head west to California, and finally he went. He'd planned to stay only for a short time, but at the last minute he changed plans and stayed to write. He drove over a bridge in Sausalito, looked to his right, and felt a great burst of energy. It was as if the place itself were calling to him. "I said to myself, 'There is something out here for me,'" Mike recalled. "'All I have to do is go.'"

Mike settled in a little town called Tiburon. There he began to work on a novel and screenplays. It was the first time in his adult life that he'd reengaged with his artistic side. Around this time Mike and I had our reading.

"These are really, really important years coming up for you," I told him. "You're going to grow so much. You've been waiting for so long, and now your time has come. There is going to be a great healing in your life. You are redefining for yourself what it means to be a man."

Even though Mike had been brave enough to reconnect with his artistic side, he still wasn't sure he was doing the right thing.

"Yes, I have gone back to being an artist," he told me, "but I haven't been all that successful. So in a way, my father was right."

"No!" I said. "This is not about you making a million dollars. This is about you embracing the journey. The success was in finally taking this path. And by doing that you are empowering yourself! You are saying, 'My voice matters! What I feel matters! Who I am matters!' That is a full victory right there."

At this point, the Other Side showed me an image of a bonsai tree, and I understood the symbolism. Bonsai trees are pretty little trees that are grown in pots that restrict their growth. The trees are clipped and shaped and twisted into the owner's design. The bonsai tree was Mike.

"You have been stunted," I told him. "You were clipped and twisted by your childhood. You were crippled and you were not allowed to grow. You never achieved self-actualization. You never understood your own energy. You never gave yourself the permission to be the person you wanted to be.

"I want you to picture a small bonsai tree," I continued. "Now I want you to picture the ground suddenly shaking and rumbling, and all of a sudden this huge tree explodes out of the ground, and this big, beautiful tree shoots up into the sky, growing as big as a redwood! And I want you to know that this tree is who you are! That is your place in the universe. You are not a bonsai tree anymore. You are growing and growing and nothing can hold you back!"

My reading with Mike went on for ninety minutes. It was clear he was still struggling, still learning, still trying to pass his soul test. But what mattered most was that he'd found the courage to face that test. For the first time in his adult life, he'd found a way to honor the essence of who he is, to honor the pull.

Best of all, Mike would not be alone on his journey. He had someone in his corner who was pulling for him.

"Your father says he's been cowardly," I told Mike. "He is sorry for what he did, but he doesn't even know where to start. He feels like he will never be able to make up for all he took from you. But he says he wants to try. He wants to help you with your art. He is on your side now."

After the reading was over, Mike sat down on his sofa and thought about his father's offer. Was he ready to let his father help him? Was he ready to forgive him? He felt a tear roll down his cheek. Then another. Then, just as suddenly, he was laughing. Then he was crying again. He sat on his sofa and laughed and cried for a long time. Emotions—emotions!—poured out of him like water.

"I was almost hysterical," he told me later. "I was just so overwhelmed by revisiting these moments from my childhood. To hear my father was sorry for what he did—to hear that this tough guy was apologizing—that was a mind-blower. My father admitting he made mistakes was what made the healing possible."

In the days after my reading with Mike, I felt the Other Side trying to push through again, rather forcefully. I was not surprised that it was Mike's father.

Mike's father had a request. Actually, it was more like a demand. He felt he hadn't done enough in the reading to convince his son of his remorse. He needed my help.

This was a very rare situation for me. It is not often that someone comes through like that, demanding help. But my reading with Mike was still very fresh in my mind, and I could sense Mike's father's desperation. And so I followed through on his request.

A few days later, Mike found two packages in his mailbox. In one, he found a small stuffed animal—a smiling blue dog. In the other, he found a small pad of drawing paper and a set of colored pencils. He stared at the contents of these packages for a long time, wondering where they had come from and what they meant. Then he found the note at the bottom of one of the packages. It read:

> Dear Mike:
> This is actually from your father. He instructed me to send
> it. He says he is sorry—that you were always a wonderful
> son but that he was too blinded by his own issues to cele-
> brate and support you in the ways that he should have. He
> didn't know how to love the right way. He's sorry for all he
> took from you. He sends you love and asks for your forgive-
> ness. He's proud of all you accomplished. Much love from
> your dad.

Mike set the items down on a table by his desk. They have stayed there ever since, inspiration for when he sits down to write. He is getting closer and closer to having something wonderful happen—he can sense it, and so can I—and he feels more encouraged than ever.

And, after a lifetime, he is ready to let his father help him on his best and highest path.

29

The QEEG

EVER SINCE THE DAYS BEFORE my grandfather's death, when I rushed out of the swimming pool, driven by an impulse I couldn't explain, I lived with the fear that there was something wrong with me. Initially, I feared that I was cursed. Over time I challenged the notion—I dug around, explored, investigated. I went to see a psychic medium, and she helped chip away at the fear. I saw a psychiatrist, who told me I wasn't crazy or broken. I submitted to two scientific tests of my abilities, and I passed them both. I was steadily moving beyond my fear.

Yet there remained one question I was desperate to answer: Was there something different about my brain?

And then, remarkably, I met someone who was able to answer that question.

At an afterlife conference in San Diego in November 2013, my friend and fellow medium Janet Mayer introduced me to Dr. Jeff Tarrant.

Jeff is a licensed psychologist who is board certified in neuro-feedback, a therapeutic tool that measures and trains brainwave activity. He taught classes in neuroscience, biofeedback, and mindfulness at the University of Missouri, and he also ran a counseling and wellness center in Columbia, Missouri. Today he lectures and is in private practice. I loved his energy from the moment I met him.

When Jeff learned that I was a psychic medium he asked to test my brain, and I agreed. We arranged a date for him to bring his equipment to New York. We met at Bob and Phran Ginsberg's home on Long Island on a cloudy morning in March 2014. Jeff set up his gear in their living room and then settled himself across the table from me while assistants took notes. "I am going to ask you to do various things," Jeff said. "Relax and think about nothing with your eyes closed, and then do the same with them open. Then we'll have you engage in psychic activity, and finally perform as a medium."

At every step, Jeff would record the electrical activity in different parts of my brain. The data would allow him to see which parts of my brain were functioning when, and to compare my brain to other, so-called normal brains. The process was called a QEEG test, which stands for "quantitative electroencephalogram"—a statistical analysis of electrical activity in the cerebral cortex, the brain's outer layer of tissue.

He helped me slip on a snug blue Electro-Cap, a spandex skullcap studded with twenty tin electrodes and connector ribbons. The electrodes, Jeff explained, were positioned according to the International 10-20 System. To me, it seemed like one of those old-fashioned swim caps, and it was so tight it felt like I was getting a facelift. He plugged the connector ribbons into an amplifier and then into his laptop.

"Okay, now I want you to just relax and do nothing," Jeff said. He might as well have asked me to hold my breath underwater for ten minutes. As I sat quietly, I could feel my "psychic door" wanting to open with letters, words, names, images, stories. I slammed the door shut and stared at a water bottle on the table, trying to focus. I sang songs in my head—"Runaround Sue," for some reason, then "This Little Light of Mine." Finally Jeff told me that this portion of the test was over. It felt like an hour; it had been three minutes.

A casual conversation was next. Again, I had to fend off intrusions from the Other Side. While I made small talk about the weather, I could feel someone's grandfather trying to push through, and someone's mother, and also a male figure whom I took to be a linguist or scientist from the nineteenth century. I figured he must have been hoping to connect with Jeff.

Finally Jeff asked me to engage in psychic activity.

"No medium stuff yet," Jeff said. "But you can go psychic crazy."

The pushy grandfather kept trying to come through, but I kept closing the door. I focused hard on the bits of information that were coming to me. The first really clear bit of information had to do with Jeff.

"You're moving," I said. "I see pine trees and a fireplace. There is something wrong with the fireplace, and there are wood floors you need to polish. Also, you're supposed to get a new prescription for your glasses."

"I just got a new one," Jeff said.

"You didn't get it right," I said. "Get another one."

There were more images for Jeff. "Hug your daughter," I told him. "She's going to have a tough road for a bit. And tell your mother she is not crazy. She was talking to her mom the other day in the shower."

Next, messages came through for the other people in the room. I turned to the woman who was taking pictures and told her that she was going to move from an apartment to a house.

Another member of Jeff's team needed to fix his diet. Yet another one had done the right thing by buying a safer car. After a while, Jeff said the psychic portion of the test was done. This time it felt like I'd only been speaking for five minutes, but the reading had gone on for twenty-one minutes.

It was now time for the medium work. The pushy grandfather finally had his say.

"Jeff, your grandfather is coming through," I said. "I'm hearing a *J* or *G* sound."

Jeff nodded.

Then I heard the name clearly. "Giuseppe. He's telling me the name Giuseppe."

Jeff seemed startled. "Yes," he said, "that was his name."

"He's telling me it's so much better for him where he is because now his wife is there with him." Then Jeff's grandmother, who had recently passed, came through. "She is showing me what she looked like when she was twenty-eight," I said. "And she is saying, 'Look at me. I was hot stuff, wasn't I?'"

Other relatives came through with messages for everyone in the room. The medium session lasted seven minutes, though to me it felt like no time at all. Before I knew it Jeff had his data, and the QEEG was done.

Back in Missouri, Jeff reviewed the data and called me with the results.

"Well," Jeff said, "the first thing I have to ask is if you've ever had any type of serious, traumatic brain injury. A car accident or major concussion?"

No, I'd never suffered any kind of brain injury.

"Here's the thing," Jeff went on. "I ran your data through what is called a TBI discriminant analysis, and it produced a 97.5 percent probability index for you. That means your brainwave patterns are almost 100 percent consistent with those of someone who has had a traumatic brain injury. Laura, parts of your brain are not behaving normally."

So there it was. My brain *was* different.

Jeff's mapping of my brain allowed him to pinpoint specific areas of abnormal brain activity. Some of it was way too technical for me to understand. For instance, Jeff informed me that in my cingulate gyrus the brainwave activity was seven standard deviations off from normal 4 Hz activity, and seven standard deviations, according to Jeff, is off the charts. Not exactly something I'd put on my resume.

But other insights produced by the brain mapping made a great deal of sense to me and shed light on exactly why I was the way I was.

Jeff showed me a readout of wave activity in different areas of my brain. During psychic activity there was a high degree of abnormal activity in the right rear portion of my brain where the parietal and temporal lobes meet (represented by the second line in the graph below). Instead of a steady series of small waves—normal, which suggests brainwave activity—Jeff recorded a series

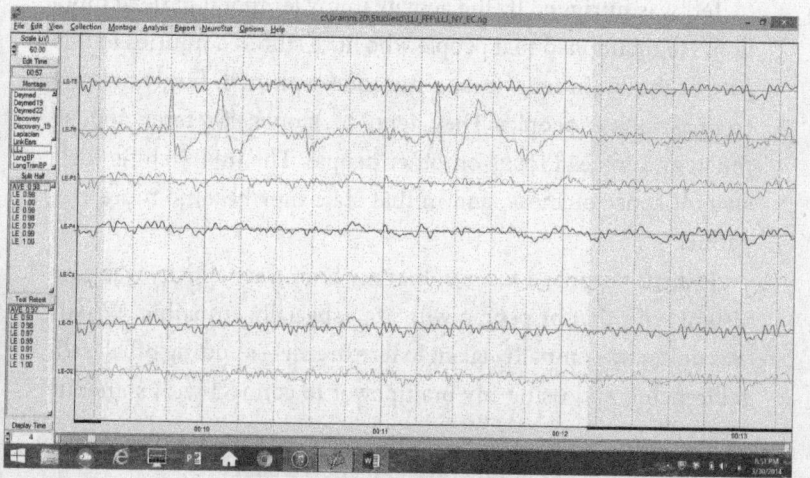

of bigger, intermittent waves, the kind usually seen in deep sleep or when a person is in a coma.

"The voltage of brainwaves is measured in microvolts, and the normal range is from zero to 60," Jeff explained. "But your activity in some areas was as high as 150 microvolts! You were blowing out the scale!"

If a neuroscientist had been shown the graph, he or she would probably conclude that the subject was having a seizure. So what was causing the abnormal activity in my brain?

Jeff explained that the temporal-parietal junction is the area of the brain associated with such functions as storing new memories, processing sensory input, deriving meaning, and emotional regulation. In other words, this part of the brain has a lot to do with defining our sense of self. For instance, when people meditate—the practice of relaxing our minds and inducing a more sedate level of consciousness—they are basically slowing down the self-referencing activity in their brains. Essentially, they are giving their ego a rest.

But I wasn't meditating. I was talking.

Jeff was intrigued by the activity in my temporal-parietal junction. He mentioned that people who have suffered injuries to this part of the brain tend to become more spiritual, forgiving, and compassionate people. They tend to stop self-referencing so much and instead focus on other people. The injury shifts their state of consciousness, and in that state they become more empathic.

I wasn't surprised to learn that my brainwave activity was consistent with that of people who are especially empathic. What I was doing was empathy taken to its extreme—shutting off all self-referencing and using my brainpower to connect with someone else.

But how did my brain enter that altered state?

"You are not asleep or unconscious or meditating, yet parts of your brain appear to be offline," Jeff said. "It's as if you're consciously getting your brain out of the way so that other people and other messages can come through. When you perform as a psychic or a medium some parts of your brain are basically not functioning, even though there's no event to explain why that's so. Somehow your brain is capable of getting into this altered state on its own."

This made sense to me. When I do a reading, my ego dissolves, and I connect with something greater than myself, something beyond my individual persona. The portal that allows for that, the test results seemed to suggest, was somewhere in my brain.

The QEEG also showed that psychic abilities occurred in one side of my brain, while medium activities occurred in another. These two distinct areas matched up with the two sides of the screen I access for readings. At the very least this showed that my perception of what was happening when I acted as a psychic or medium was not just some weird reality I invented—it was actually reflected in my brain. Events were occurring in my brain that I couldn't possibly control or invent.

But did the QEEG answer the question of why I was the way I was? And did it prove I was actually receiving information from the Other Side?

"The only real way to prove you're getting what you say you're getting from the Other Side is through the information you relay," Jeff said. "Is it accurate? Is it something you couldn't possibly know? That's something people have to decide for themselves." In other words, my brain mapping only proved something abnormal was happening in my brain. What it didn't do was give a name to what that something was.

There was one final piece of information from the brain mapping session I'd like to share.

Jeff concluded that my brain has the capacity to handle and process the flow of information I receive in a reading. He couldn't see what I saw—no one could—but he could be certain that what I saw was being processed by my brain. The mysterious machine that is the human brain has, in my case, a system, a structure—a fully functioning mechanism—to process the visual stimuli that occur when I engage as a psychic or a medium. That mechanism exists. It is real.

And because my brain is basically the same as everyone else's—it's not an alien brain or a cyborg brain, it's a standard human brain—it is possible, Jeff reasoned, that this mechanism exists in all our brains.

"Maybe we all have it," Jeff said. "Maybe in the future we'll be able to teach people how to get into the altered state you are able to enter. Maybe it will be something we'll be able to develop for ourselves. There's a lot about the brain we still don't understand."

I, for one, believe this mechanism—this switch—exists in every one of us. I don't know why it's more pronounced and functional in me, but I do believe we are all capable of slowing down our self-referential activity and allowing more information from other sources to come through. I believe we're all capable of focusing more of our thought energy outside ourselves and onto other people, and in that way we can become more empathic.

And I believe that when we question and explore how we fit into the universe, we can overcome the fears and doubts that keep us from discovering our highest path.

30

Entanglement

ON A BUSY STREET in Manhattan on the morning of November 20, 2012, a complicated boy named Kyle rode his skateboard downtown from Penn Station to Greenwich Village.

Kyle grew up on Long Island, an extremely bright, beautiful child with boundless energy and curiosity. He was also hard to control—not because he was bad, but because he was stubborn. As he got older, Kyle withdrew; he found socializing with other kids difficult. He had a handful of friends, and he was a talented musician—he played the clarinet and saxophone, was a competitive drummer, and sang with an a capella group. But he was most comfortable being by himself.

His parents took him to doctors and searched for answers, but there was never a definitive diagnosis. Depression, anxiety, a mood disorder—no one knew what exactly troubled Kyle. The thing is, he was highly functioning. It's just that he marched to the beat of a different drummer.

Eventually Kyle gave up on trying to fit into a world in which he felt like an outcast. He believed he'd never be accepted anyway, so he stopped trying.

Not surprisingly, Kyle's view of the world grew darker, too. He didn't see it as a good and beautiful place; he saw it as hypercritical and judgmental. He had many people who loved him, but he had a hard time believing in the goodness of people. His connection to the world started to fade. He felt shut out, isolated, ignored. Despite having loving, concerned parents, he believed he was alone.

And yet he did not give up. He kept trying to make the pieces fit. He enrolled at New York University and worked hard to be a good student. On November 19, 2012, he stayed up late finishing a paper that was due the next day. The next morning, he took the train into Manhattan.

One of the most important lessons the Other Side tries to teach us is the reality that we are all connected as spiritual beings. But if that's true, where does someone like Kyle fit in?

Kyle did not feel like a part of that connectedness. He could see no evidence of it in his life; instead he saw a fragmented, fend-for-yourself world. In his experience, people could be mean, unfeeling, hurtful. He saw no point in forging connections that would likely result in pain. Instead he accepted that he was alone in this life.

But was he really alone?

If a universal spiritual connection truly exists, why was Kyle on the outside of it? What good is such a connection if it isn't all-encompassing—if someone like Kyle can feel excluded from it? And what if Kyle was right? What if we aren't invested in one another's joy and success and growth? What if, in our journey through life, we are, in fact, ultimately alone?

The Other Side teaches us that we are never alone.

Scientists grapple with this question, too—are the various facets of existence moving through time and space alone, or is there some subtle, unseen force that binds them all together? This has led scientists to explore a phenomenon called entanglement.

In his book *Entangled Minds*, Dean Radin, a senior scientist at the Institute of Noetic Sciences, writes about an experiment that explored the relationship of photons—subatomic particles of electromagnetic radiation—to each other. The experiment showed that certain photons are connected in ways that we aren't yet able to explain.

For instance, subatomic particles such as electrons or photons that are created in the same event have measurable properties such as spin or polarization that reveal them to be intimately linked together no matter how far apart they become. Their resulting connection, as revealed in increasingly refined experiments over recent decades, confirms the shocking reality of what Einstein referred to as "spooky actions at a distance," because this intimate connection reveals the particles to remain linked together in complete violation of common sense and of Einstein's notion of the speed of light as the ultimate speed at which information (or the effect of one particle on another) can travel. Measurement of one particle instantaneously affects the other. The implications for the complete interconnectedness of the entire universe, and for our very understanding of the fundamental nature of space and time, are profound. That is entanglement.

Put simply, entanglement implies that "at very deep levels the separations we see between ordinary, isolated objects are, in a sense, illusions created by our limited perceptions," Radin writes. "Physical reality is connected in ways we're just beginning to understand."

Visually, the Other Side has shown me a massive field of light energy, not unlike the sun. This field is unified, but it is also distinctly made up of billions and billions of smaller points of light, like a single image that, on close inspection, is made up of hundreds of smaller images. These billions of points of light are us.

What I see is that we comprise the massive field of light—it cannot exist without us. But neither can we individually exist outside this field. Our existence is primarily defined by our place in this grand constellation of energy, not by who we are individually. We may appear to exist separately from anyone else, and we may perceive the boundaries that describe us and feel we are autonomous. But our energy, our consciousness, is inexorably entangled with the energy of others.

Here is another analogy: Picture a hand with five fingers. Each finger is distinct, but each finger also connects to the same source—the hand itself. The fingers are separate, but connected. We as humans have vastly different experiences here on earth, but all of our experiences funnel into one massive collective experience—the experience of our existence.

Our souls, ourselves, our experiences, our existence—these are not isolated in any way. The universe is not a place of separateness, it is a place of entanglement. We are connected to others in ways we cannot fathom.

On November 20, Kyle's train into Manhattan was cancelled due to track damage, so he had to take a later train to the city. He texted his father about the delay—"This is so stupid. I'm going to be late"—but he made it into Penn Station by 11:00 a.m. Then he hopped on his skateboard and headed down Broadway. When he got to Union Square Park, he veered onto Union Square West. Suddenly, a bicycle messenger came racing toward him from the wrong direction just as a large truck was passing him on his left. There was a collision. Kyle was knocked off his skateboard and lay motionless on the street.

A few hours later, when his mother, Nancy, got home, there was a message from a police officer. All he said was, "Please call me."

That night, Kyle's family went to see his body in the morgue. "It was all so surreal," Nancy said. "He was just twenty years old."

A few months after Kyle's funeral, Nancy called me. She'd heard about me from a friend, Dr. Marc Reitman—the psychiatrist who had helped me embrace my gift. Dr. Reitman thought I might be able to help Nancy.

In our reading, Kyle came through right away, strongly and clearly. He wanted to talk about what happened.

"He is showing me a vehicle and impact, but he is also showing me that he wasn't in the vehicle," I told her. "He is also showing me it wasn't his fault. He is showing me people standing over him in the street, a person holding his hand, holding his head. He says this was important for him because in his final moments here, he crossed surrounded by people who were concerned for him. He wasn't alone. Someone held him as he crossed."

On the other end of the phone, Nancy was crying. She told me the story of Kyle's accident.

"It happened across from a McDonald's," she said. "A young man was coming out of the McDonald's, and if he'd kept walking he would have been gone when the accident happened. But he dropped something and he had to go back to pick it up. And when he did, the accident happened. Right in front of him."

Nancy had tracked the man down and learned more about those crucial moments.

"His first instinct was to run away," she said. "But something kept him there. Something pulled him toward the street. He was the first bystander to make his way to Kyle."

Nancy told me the young man knelt beside Kyle and held him

in his arms. He noticed someone try to take Kyle's skateboard, and with one arm he grabbed him and stopped him. He saw someone else start to take a photo with their phone, and he stopped them, too. "He felt like he'd been placed there to protect my son," Nancy told me. "He stayed with him until the ambulance came."

Kyle was still conscious when the man first got to him. For a moment he was able to look up into the eyes of this stranger, who held him even tighter. Then Kyle's eyes rolled back in his head.

"Another woman was there, too, kneeling next to Kyle," Nancy said. "She also stayed with him until the ambulance came. A lot of people lingered nearby. They formed a sort of circle around him."

"Kyle is bringing up this young man for a reason," I told Nancy. "He is bringing him up because he knows the man was there out of the goodness of his heart. He knows this man didn't want to be there, but he stayed anyway. He stayed because he is kind. And Kyle could see the goodness in him."

Kyle had so much more to say. He told his mother he was happy now—that he no longer had to work so hard to make all the pieces fit. He said he was with his grandfather, Pops, whom he adored. And he said he understood things now in a way he never had on earth.

In the weeks after Kyle's passing, Nancy came to see Kyle in a new light, too. It started when one of Kyle's high school classmates—someone who was also struggling—came to her and told her that Kyle had made a big difference in her life. "She had experienced family problems that made her afraid," Nancy said, "and Kyle made her feel like it was going to be okay. He gave her his friendship. He was there for her."

More friends approached Nancy and told her similar stories. The boy who fought with his parents and got kicked out of his house—Kyle had brought him home so he'd have a place to sleep.

The boy who was dabbling in harder and harder drugs—Kyle had talked him away from the really dangerous stuff. "So many kids, the ones who weren't popular, the ones who were in the shadows— they were the ones who came up to me and told me how much Kyle meant to them," Nancy told me. "It was as if Kyle was giving to others the very thing he himself had been searching for."

In Kyle's journal, Nancy found a quote that struck her as particularly poignant:

> To the world you may be one person
> But to one person, you may be the world

"Kyle copied that quote, so he must have believed it on some level, but it was as if he couldn't convince himself that he was an important part of so many lives," she said. "And then he came through in the reading, and he finally realized he wasn't alone, and he finally saw his own goodness, and he finally understood his place in the world. And that is the big lesson of Kyle's story. Never feel that one person can't change someone else's life."

My reading with Kyle and his mother has stayed with me in a very powerful way. The lesson Kyle learned in the final moments of his life on earth is so profoundly beautiful. Many people face hardships and obstacles, and sometimes they push away the people who love them. Kyle's struggles made him feel alone. And then, in the most tragic of circumstances, he accepted someone's love, and in that instant he learned he had never really been alone.

Nancy told me that when she spoke to the bystander she'd learned he'd led a difficult life and had problems of his own. He, too, had doubts about his place in the world. Then he witnessed the accident, and he cradled Kyle, easing Kyle's passage from this world to the next. And something in him changed. That remarkable moment of connectedness began to heal the young man, too.

To me, that is better evidence of our interconnected existence than any scientific experiment could ever provide. We are all connected. We are all entangled. We are all invested in each other's fates and fortunes.

In my reading with Nancy, Kyle mentioned a ring. He kidded her about not changing the sheets on his bed—she'd left his bedroom untouched for months—and he told her that when she finally cleaned it up, she should look for the ring. Nancy had no idea what he was talking about. But a week later, when she went through Kyle's things, she found a small silver ring with tiny black hearts painted on the inside of the band. She slipped it on her ring finger, and it fit perfectly. She hasn't taken it off since.

Nancy has also started a scholarship in Kyle's name. It is awarded to the student who best exemplifies what it means to be a leader. "It's for the kid who's always there to help someone else," Nancy said.

Through the scholarship, and through the many friends he touched during his short life, Kyle lives on. Down on Union Square West, on the sidewalk next to the scene of the accident, a small vase with flowers sits beneath a tree. Every Sunday, Nancy or her husband visits the site and puts fresh flowers in the vase. In December, there's a small Christmas tree. Sometimes strangers stop and ask them who the flowers are for, and they tell them the story of Kyle.

"And then these strangers, when I see them again, they stop me and say hello," Nancy said. "And they tell me, 'Every day when we walk by this tree, we say hello to Kyle.' They didn't even know him, and yet they talk to him every day. And to know Kyle's name is still out there, still in the air, what a gift that is. Because Kyle wasn't alone then, and he isn't alone now."

None of us are.

31

The Swimming Pool

AT 7:05 A.M. I pulled into the parking lot of Herricks High School, where I'd been teaching for sixteen years. I parked in my assigned parking spot, beneath a shady tree near the back entrance. I walked down the first-floor hallway where the seniors have their lockers. My outfit was unexceptional—beige pants, orange top, orange cardigan (orange is my favorite color), laminated ID on a lanyard around my neck. I carried a thermos of coffee. So why was everyone staring at me?

Some students I knew, some I didn't, a couple of teachers—pretty much everyone stopped what they were doing and looked at me, little knowing smiles on their faces. I kept walking, wondering what was going on.

I ducked into the English Department office and went over my notes on teaching rhetorical strategy using *Narrative of the Life of Frederick Douglass*. At 7:25 a.m. the first bell rang and I headed to room 207. Normally the students are still half asleep, but today they were alert, waiting in their seats for me to arrive. There was a weird, crackling energy in the room. I ignored the attention and pushed on with my lesson plan.

At 8:14 the bell rang. No one bolted for the door, as they usually do. Every student stayed put. Finally, one of them, a smart, outgoing kid named Owen, seated in the back row, said, "Mrs. Jackson? Are you psychic?"

I heard someone gasp.

Stunned, I said, "I'm sorry, what?"

"Are you psychic?" Owen repeated. "Are you a psychic medium?"

I just stood there, speechless. This was it. The moment I'd been dreading.

I realized pretty quickly how it had happened. One of the people I regularly read for is a famous pop singer—a young, dynamic star who has a huge following on social media. Just a few nights earlier she'd invited me to her concert at the Barclays Center in Brooklyn, where she was opening for an even more famous pop star. Afterward, in her dressing room, I posed for a photo with her.

She posted the photo to Instagram, thanking me and identifying me as Laura Lynne Jackson. No one at the high school knew me by my full name. When some of my students saw the photo of the famous pop star with their English teacher, they Googled me and found the website describing my abilities as a psychic medium.

"You kinda blew up our social media last night, Mrs. Jackson," is how one student put it.

After I got over the shock of being outed I was ready to answer Owen's question. It was something I'd rehearsed with the principal.

"Yes, I am a psychic medium," I said. "I've been tested by scientific researchers who have verified my abilities. But this part of my life is separate from my job as a teacher. So beyond answering your question, Owen, I won't take up any more class time discussing it further. You don't have to worry that I'm reading you in the classroom, and I won't read for anyone in any of my classes, so don't even ask. It's not appropriate for us to take up any more time with this."

"Can you tell when someone's cheating on a test?" one student asked.

The truth was, I could. During a test the month before, I had been sitting at my desk, with my back momentarily to the students, quickly taking attendance on the computer. Suddenly I felt an energy lasso pulling me to the rear of the classroom. It felt like a hand on my arm yanking me to turn around. I followed the pull and saw a boy in the last row trying to hide a slip of paper under his hand. I walked over to him and asked for the paper, now hidden under his leg. "That's cheating," I told him. "You know better than that."

Still, I wasn't about to share that story with my students, and I repeated that we wouldn't be spending any more time on the subject, but the questions kept coming.

"What is heaven like?"

"Is my dog in heaven?"

"Can I talk to my grandmother in heaven?"

"Can you read minds?"

"Have you ever worked on a missing-person case?"

I realized my students were drawn to ask about my abilities because they were living open, questioning lives! I had figured most of the kids would want to know more about the pop star, and certainly plenty of them did, but what surprised me most was how fascinated they were by my gift.

I wanted very badly to answer their questions, but I knew I couldn't. Instead I quickly shut the discussion down and shooed the students to their next class.

This same scenario played out over the next six periods. In my last class of the day, period eight, I gave my speech about keeping my work as a psychic medium apart from my work as a teacher. Again I resisted the urge to share my views about the Other Side and respond to their curiosity. So I made my statement and sent them to their next class. But one student refused to leave.

She was fifteen years old, pretty, and very smart, but also shy and quiet. After everyone left she stood by her desk and covered her face with her hands, but I could see that she was crying. Then she shuffled to the front of the room.

"Mrs. Jackson," she said in the barest whisper, "I need your help."

A few months earlier, her mother had remarried after many years alone. Her new stepfather was a loving, caring man who doted on both her and her mother and brought much joy and happiness to their lives. But then, just three weeks after the wedding, he went for a swim in their backyard pool. Suddenly she heard her mother screaming.

The girl ran outside and saw her stepfather floating facedown in the deep end of the pool. Her mother couldn't swim, so she was screaming for the girl to jump in and save her stepfather.

"But I froze," my student said, crying harder now. "I couldn't move. I was paralyzed. I was just so scared to go into the pool. So I never did."

By the time the paramedics arrived, her stepfather was gone.

I felt this young woman's pain, guilt, and torment deep in my soul. It was heartbreaking. She waited for me to say something, anything, but I didn't know what to say. I wasn't supposed to read my students. I'd just explained that I would never cross that line. But this girl's burden was staggering. And I knew it could define her life if she was forced to carry it forever.

"Can you please tell him that I'm sorry?" she said. "Please?"

What was I supposed to do?

In fact, I was already reading her. The door had swung open and her stepfather came through forcefully. He made it clear that it was not her fault. *Please tell her it was not her fault.*

I hesitated. I'd spent the last two decades keeping my two paths separate. I'd carefully maintained my double life. And now the wall I'd put up was coming down. Would I be able to put it back up?

"It was just his time," I finally said. "You would not have been able to save your stepfather even if you did go in the pool. I feel his heart gave out, and that's why he didn't make it. You couldn't have saved him. It was just his time. It was never your fault."

The girl stopped crying and looked at me, holding her breath. Her eyes were big and wide and her lips were trembling. "There is something else your stepfather wants you to know, and this is very important," I told her. "He wants you to know that his greatest gift—the greatest gift he ever got in his whole life—was getting to meet your mother, and getting to meet you, and getting to spend time with you both. And he wants to thank you for that. He says you gave him a beautiful gift."

The girl burst into tears. I put my hand on her shoulder. My two worlds were colliding, and I wasn't able to stop it.

I wasn't sure anymore if I should even try.

32

Angel Way

I WAS DRIVING to see my friend Bobbi Allison on Long Island. I glanced at my car's navigation screen just as it told me to get off at the next exit.

Wow, that exit came up quicker than I'd expected, I thought. The whole trip had taken just seventeen minutes; I'd assumed I'd be driving a lot longer than that. Still, I followed the GPS and took the next exit.

Bobbi is one of my closest psychic medium friends, and I was going to see her for lunch in her new apartment. I couldn't wait to experience the energy she had created in her new space. The navigation told me I'd be there in just a few minutes. Then it told me to take a sharp right, then a sharp left, then another two rights. Weird. It seemed that I was circling the outskirts of a neighborhood right next to the expressway.

"You have arrived at your destination," the voice of the navigation system announced.

But how could that be? There wasn't a house in sight! "You have arrived at your destination," the navigation system repeated sternly.

I called Bobbi on my cell.

"Um, I'm confused," I told her. "My navigation took me on a wild-goose chase and left me on a street right off an exit on the expressway. Do you live around here?"

"What's the street name?" Bobbi asked.

I looked up at the sign.

"Angel Way," I said.

Bobbi burst out laughing.

"Are you kidding me?" she said. "No, I don't live there, but I know where it is. You're about twenty minutes away. But Laura, that is so funny! The spirits must be having a little fun with us! Angel Way! Too funny!"

I laughed, too. The Other Side, it seems, does have a sense of humor. I'd known for a long time that the Other Side can manipulate things that run on electricity, either to get us a message or, in this case, to have some fun with us. And now I learned not to depend too heavily on my navigation system again.

Strange and wonderful things seem to happen when I get together with my psychic medium friends. There is a heightened energy that crackles among us. But the best thing is that we get it—we all know what it's like to be "weird" and perceive things in unconventional ways, and we understand the great responsibility of having these heightened abilities. We commiserate over the exhaustion that comes with doing readings. We compare the boundaries we set between our "normal" lives and our psychic lives. Together, we find a level of comfort, support, and understanding that we don't have anywhere else.

Years ago, we began to meet about once a month for a psychic girls' night out—or as we like to jokingly call it, "a witches' brew." Sometimes that whole gang will show up: Bobbi, Kim Russo,

Bethe Altman, Diana Cinquemani, all psychic mediums; Pat Longo, a spiritual healer and teacher; and the fabulous Dorene Bair, an intuitive "change agent," as the title on her business card reads. Our get-togethers are something to behold. Let's just say our spirits run high. Alcohol, as I've mentioned, seems to open our abilities more. And from there, the energy just builds.

We held one of our recent brews—Kim, Bobbi, and I—at Fanatico, an Italian restaurant in Hicksville, Long Island, one of my favorites. We sat at a table near the front and ordered pasta with Brussels sprouts and olives, some spaghetti squash marinara, and two plates of the crowd favorite, burnt broccoli. Kim and Bobbi ordered wine and I had a Grey Goose Cosmo.

Our conversation, as always, was easy and funny and casual—and pretty much about the same kind of stuff any three friends would talk about. Bobbi told us about her daughter's new home in South Carolina and how it was such a great deal.

"How much?" Kim asked in disbelief. "There are purses that cost more than that."

We talked about how our work is endlessly rewarding but also pretty tiring. We had to be careful not to be "on" all the time or we'd get physically sick. I mentioned how I'd done several readings and one big group reading in quick succession, and ended up with the flu and whooping cough, which put me out of commission for three months. Bobbi said she was just getting over a nasty case of bronchitis because she had recently overdone it.

We came to realize that while we all operated on the same vibration, as Kim put it, we also had different techniques.

"I see tangible spirits in front of me," Kim explained.

"I do, too," Bobbi said.

"That's never happened to me," I said.

I mentioned how I get information from the Other Side on an internal screen divided into specific sections. Neither Kim nor Bobbi had ever used a screen.

"I use automatic writing," Bobbi said, discussing her ability to write down thoughts and insights from the Other Side without being conscious of what she's writing. That, too, was unfamiliar to me.

We came to our profession in different ways. Kim and Bobbi both had teachers who'd mentored them, while I'd developed on my own. That reminded Bobbi about the first psychic healing class she ever took.

"I was afraid to go," she said. "I was afraid of what I'd encounter. I thought I was going to see chickens running around with their heads cut off."

Of course, there were no headless chickens. And Bobbi loved the class.

Kim recalled how she and her sister attended a presentation by a psychic named Holly. This woman invited Kim to take her class, which consisted of the basic principles of developing one's intuition, and told her she was already an advanced psychic medium. She then recommended Kim learn the basics of grounding and protection and informed her that her spirit guides would teach her the rest.

"A medium," Kim told us she asked, "how do you know that?"

"Honey, I'm psychic, remember," Holly said.

At our dinners we read for each other, since we're all so tuned into each other's energy. And invariably, when we get our reading, one of us will say, "How did you know that?" before quickly laughing at the absurdity of the question.

"Something happened with your car today, didn't it?" Bobbi might say.

"How did you know that?" Kim will ask.

"Honey, I'm psychic."

We give each other advice, too, based on what we're seeing from the Other Side.

"When one of you read for me, it's an enormous validation,"

Bobbi said. "It's usually about something I was thinking but wasn't sure about."

"That's because it's hard for us to get information about ourselves," Kim said. "Like right now, I know something is happening in my life but I'm not being shown anything. Anything! And I am respecting that, because I don't want to be a brat and say, 'Come on, I wanna know!'"

"When I read for you guys, I go to the left side of my screen, which is where I see the spirit guides," I said. "That's where a person's guides always hang out. And the guides give me messages for you."

"It's like our spirit guides are all in this together," Bobbi said.

Spirit guides are souls who have lived on earth before (but not during our current lifetime) and are now continuing their journeys on the Other Side. And as part of their journeys, they have jobs—just as we do here on earth. Those jobs are meant to help them learn the lessons they need to learn so that they, too, can move forward in their journeys. These souls become spirit guides, and being spirit guides helps them grow. They are our protectors, teachers, mentors, and cheerleaders. They put thoughts in our heads and send us nudges, signs, affirmations, creative impulses, brainstorms, instincts, gut feelings. When we talk about honoring our pull, they are the ones who are pulling. They always want us to find our best path.

Bobbi was right. Our spirit guides were working together.

"They all know each other," I said. "Our spirit guides are all on the same team."

That night at Fanatico, we started getting information for each other.

"I'm getting a lot of stuff for you," I told Kim. "Good stuff."

"The guides are telling me they're working things out behind the scenes, but that's all I know," said Kim, who was in the middle of an important career decision.

"They are showing me that you have to stop pushing and let it go," I said. "The last year, it's all been push, push, push, and you have to let it go. They are controlling how things unfold. There's a reason for that. There is a plan in place. Letting go will be a difficult feeling for a while, but you just have to do it to allow your best path to unfold for you."

"Well, as I'm walking my path, they're not giving me any hints at all," Kim said.

"Here's a hint they're letting me see," I said. "I'm seeing Los Angeles. Definitely Los Angeles. You are going to find you are pulled to Los Angeles, and there will be a show that you are part of that is going to unfold, just as they have planned. You just have to honor your pulls and just show up. They will make it happen."

"For me, it's about manifesting," Kim said—referring to the practice of visualizing your goal and, through the energy of your conviction, making it happen. "We act as if it's already happened. We thank the universe for what is rightfully ours."

I told them how I manifest things—by writing a letter to the universe at the start of every year. In the letter, I thank the universe for helping me accomplish several specific goals, even though they hadn't happened yet.

"I have Pat Longo to credit for getting me to do that so clearly," I explained. "She's the one who told me I must write it down. I used to think just projecting your thoughts was enough, but she said no, there is a power in writing that matters. And she's right."

"I prove that to my husband all the time," Kim said. "He'll say, 'You can't make all that happen,' and I'll say, 'Just watch me.' And when it happens, he just shakes his head."

We laughed and talked about how the men in our lives have a camaraderie all their own. Sometimes we'll all go out together, and the husbands will wait patiently while we find a table with an energy that suits us. The men exchange knowing smiles; they understand we have to get seats that "feel right" to us.

That night , we girls closed down Fanatico. We left as the cleaning crew was kicking into gear. This tends to happen whenever we get together—hours pass in what seems like minutes.

On the way home, I wound down from the spectacular energy of our dinner and thanked the universe for bringing me such special friends. The dinner reinforced, as it always does, how connected we are to each other—and how much we need those connections. We all have a huge support team that keeps us on the right path and pushes us to be better. We have our loved ones who have crossed, and we have our spirit guides.

But we also have the people who love us and need us here on earth. And sometimes their support is the most crucial support of all. That doesn't just go for my psychic sisters and me. That goes for all of us.

33

The Light at the End

WHEN I'M NOT DEALING with the Other Side, my life is pretty ordinary. Basically, it's all about my family. To them, I'm just Mom or Sis or Blondie (that's what Garrett calls me). The funny thing is, while the Other Side will pass me incredibly specific information about complete strangers, I cannot reliably read for my family members. I know them too well, love them so much. Because I always want everything for them to be happy and smooth, I don't always trust myself to interpret the information I get from the Other Side "cleanly," without inserting my own feelings into it. That's one of the quirks of my gift—I can't always use it to help my family or myself. Which is probably for the best.

My older sister, Christine, who has four beautiful young boys, takes my gift in stride. When we get together, my abilities don't come up all that often, but occasionally the Other Side will push through with bits of information. For instance, Christine will mention a friend, and I'll suddenly say, "Does your friend have a brother named Ted?" She'll then stop the discussion and ask, "Is this a conversation or a reading?"

Even so, my sister tells me that what I do has changed the way she looks at the world. She always believed there was a heaven, but now she says she thinks it's a lot closer than the big blue sky. She believes it is right here with us. She believes we are surrounded by energy from people who have passed.

My brother, John, hasn't been quite as open to that way of thinking. He's said that he believes I have an intuitive gift, but he just can't quite commit to the idea that the Other Side is real. John is married with three kids. When something major happens in their lives, his wife will say, "Call your sister! Ask her about this!" John doesn't stand in the way of me trying to connect his family to the Other Side. And strangely, I seem to get consistently clear information for him. For instance, once I told him that a big opportunity in Asia was coming his way in three months. John, who is crazy smart and works in the tech industry, had no dealings in Asia. But right on schedule the opportunity happened, and John found himself on a plane to Korea.

At home, my abilities don't surface that often. But I do remember watching the Super Bowl with Garrett and the kids a couple of years ago. I noticed Garrett was distracted by something, and I blurted out, "Hey, you better look at the screen—you don't want to miss this touchdown that's about to happen." Three seconds later, a player intercepted a pass and ran down the field for a spectacular touchdown.

"You better hope the Mafia doesn't find out about you," Garrett said.

I'm often asked if any of my children share my gift. My oldest daughter, Ashley, one of the kindest souls I've ever known, seems to have clear psychic abilities. She feels things and reads people's energy really well. There are times when she seems to know what has yet to occur. On Mother's Day a few years ago Ashley and Garrett were driving home from a bunch of errands when Ashley suddenly said, "Mommy is going to call in ten, nine, eight, seven . . . ," and counted down all the way to one. When she got to one, Garrett's cellphone rang. It was me.

Hayden, my middle child, is a loving, energetic boy. He has something different going on: he is able to locate lost things. His gift comes in handy.

"Hayden, do you know where the TV remote is?" one of us will ask.

He'll go quiet for a moment or two, then he'll say, "In the sofa," or "Under the bed."

It works for ballet slippers, too. Last spring I told him, "Hayden, it's an emergency—we have to leave for Juliet's recital in five minutes and we can't find her other ballet shoe! Tune in! Find it!"

"Okay, give me a minute," he said, looking up and off to his right.

After just a few seconds, he got up, opened the hall closet, and started reaching deep into a dark corner.

"Hayden, it's not in there," I said—just as he pulled a ballet slipper out from behind a storage bin and waved it in the air.

On the downside, Easter egg hunts are never fair when Hayden is around. Neither is playing Battleship.

My youngest child, Juliet, is as full of light and free-spirited as I was at her young age. Everywhere we go, it seems, people are drawn to her energy. Without fail, they come over and give her things for free. It's become a running joke in our family—what will Juliet get today?

One day when she was just three, she came up to me and said, "Mommy, there's a little blond boy hanging around me."

For a second I froze. Was this just a case of an imaginary friend, or was it . . . something else?

"Well," I said, "is the boy nice or mean?"

"He's very nice," Juliet said.

"Okay," I said. "Then I guess he can stay."

Juliet smiled and skipped away to resume her beautifully innocent life.

═

Roscoe—our loyal and loving white miniature Schnauzer—was another beloved member of the family. When our last two children were born and we brought them home, Roscoe would lie at the foot of our bed and stay awake all night to keep an eye on the baby. Once he even scared away burglars with his barking. He was an awesome friend and family member.

When he was ten years old, he suddenly had a seizure. I raced him to the vet, who said it was a fluke, nothing to worry about, and sent us back home. But that didn't feel right to me. So an hour later I took him for a second opinion. This vet was concerned and ran some tests.

While I was in the waiting room with Roscoe at the vet's office, I suddenly saw the presence of another animal on the screen where I see the Other Side. I wasn't trying to read or contact anyone, the animal just appeared. I recognized her—it was Thunder, my mother's beloved black Lab, who'd crossed two years earlier. She and Roscoe had been great friends. Thunder came bounding up to the veil—the diaphanous boundary that separates this world from the Other Side on my screen—as if she were excited about something, and I knew what that meant. I had seen it before. Roscoe was going to cross imminently, and Thunder had come to greet him.

The truth is, as distraught as I was about Roscoe's sudden turn of health, the notion of him crossing wasn't a total surprise to me. A few months earlier, the Other Side had shown me that Roscoe would be crossing soon. The time frame I saw was three months. I had hoped desperately that I was wrong—that somehow I'd gotten the message mixed up. After all, Roscoe had gotten a clean bill of health at his last checkup. Even so, I told Garrett at the time, and I began to prepare myself emotionally for Roscoe's passing. Garrett and I talked it over and decided to gently prepare the kids. "Roscoe may only have a few more months with us," we told them, "so let's really value our time with him." Three months later, Roscoe had his seizure.

The X-rays showed that Roscoe had a tumor in his stomach and was bleeding internally. The vet rushed him into emergency care, and we weighed the options. Operating on Roscoe was one of them, but he was clearly in bad shape, and it seemed like we'd be subjecting him to great risk without the promise that it would help. Roscoe's body had gone into shock and we were told that there was a good chance that he would cross during surgery, without us there beside him. I remembered what the Other Side had told me. It had been three months. And I knew that Thunder was there to cross Roscoe. I understood: it was his time to go. Together, we made a decision. We would put Roscoe to sleep.

Garrett, the kids, and I were all there with him when he crossed. Each of us had a hand on his fur. We told him how much we loved him and thanked him for being such a beautiful, beautiful part of our lives. His gentle brown eyes looked into ours. And then he closed them and crossed, surrounded by our love.

Even though the Other Side had tried to prepare me for Roscoe's crossing, it was devastating. I knew his passing was part of the universe's plan for him, but still, I was overcome with sorrow. Despite all I knew about the Other Side, I still missed my lovely dog and wondered if he was okay.

The vet told us we could get Roscoe's paw print, and we all liked the idea. We waited while they made the print. I sat numbly, staring at the wall across from me. At last I focused on the poster hanging on the wall—and I gasped. It was a picture of an ant-eater.

What's so special about a poster of an anteater in a vet's office?

Long ago, I asked the Other Side to send me signs from my loved ones who've crossed. I used to ask for monarch butterflies, but after a while I decided to kick it up a notch. I began asking for three signs in particular—unusual signs. If the universe wanted to get me a message, I asked it to show me an armadillo. Or an aardvark. Or an anteater.

Why would a vet have a big picture of an anteater in his clinic? Beats me. But I know I was meant to see that anteater, and I know why. It was letting me know that Roscoe had safely arrived on the Other Side, that he was still with me, and that we were connected by love.

A moment or two later, Hayden and Juliet had to go to the bathroom. I walked them to the restroom and waited for them outside. I turned to my left, and right there, at eye level, was a small ceramic statue of a dog. A white miniature Schnauzer. The dog looked just like Roscoe, and he was smiling. The dog was happy. And on his back was a pair of angel's wings.

Okay, some will say, big deal, just a coincidence. But I know that's not what it was.

The next day, I had the nerve to ask Roscoe for yet another sign.

"Just let me know you're okay up there," I said aloud while I was driving. "Let me know by letting me hear the word *angel*."

As soon as I asked Roscoe for the sign, I turned on the car radio. A ballad was playing, and the first lyric I heard was ". . . must have been an angel."

But still—still—I didn't feel all that better. I mean, a million songs have the word *angel* in them, right?

Later that day I called the vet's office to square away our bill. The woman who answered the phone was so patient and kind as she explained the various charges. She told me how sorry she was that Roscoe had passed, and she made me feel better about everything. At the end of our conversation, I thanked her and asked for her name.

"My name is Angel," she said.

I smiled. Leave it to Roscoe to give me another sign just when I needed it most.

It was our deep, powerful love for Roscoe that kept this channel of communication open between us. It was also that love that brought me the premonition that Roscoe was going to pass, and the visit from Thunder. Many years earlier, when I was pulled out of a swimming pool by a powerful urge to see Pop Pop just weeks before he crossed, I didn't understand what a premonition was. And when Pop Pop passed, I hated somehow knowing in advance. But with Roscoe, I embraced my premonition. I knew where the message was coming from, and I understood it was driven by love. The Other Side operates only out of love. With Roscoe, the Other Side gave us the great blessing of being able to cherish and celebrate our endless love for him.

And I understand, as well as I understand anything, that Roscoe didn't leave us. Our lovely, beautiful Roscoe is still here.

=

We weren't the only ones in the family to have a profound encounter with the Other Side involving a dog. Not long ago my brother, John, learned that his beloved rescue pit bull, Boo Radley, was sick. She'd been treated for jaw cancer in the past, but now the cancer had returned and spread. There was nothing they could do to stop it. She would need to be put down.

Boo held a special place in my brother's heart. He got her after he moved to California and broke up with his girlfriend. Boo was there when he met his wife, Natasha, and when each of his three children was born: Maya, Zoey, and little Johnny. And she showered them all with love.

My brother struggled with what to tell Maya, who was just six.

He knew she would ask where Boo had gone. He wanted to prepare her for the loss and help her through it, but how could he say Boo was going to heaven when he didn't really believe it?

He turned to our mother for guidance. She believes in heaven but understood that my brother was unsure, so she suggested he tell Maya that "some people" believe there's a heaven that is beautiful and happy, that everyone—even dogs—is loved there, and that when we go there, we'll be reunited with our dogs.

John took her advice. When he told this to Maya, she said, "Daddy, are you one of the people who believe that?"

"I don't know it for sure," John told her, "but I sure hope it's true."

Boo was put to sleep the week before Christmas. John held her while she crossed. My brother ached over her loss and began to question his own thinking.

"If this is really real," he said to Boo, "if there really is a heaven, I need you to give me a sign. But it can only come from one person—Laura Lynne."

He thought of Boo's collar and said, "Boo, I want the sign to be a star with a circle around it. Get me that through Laura Lynne, and I'll believe." John told no one about the sign.

A few days later my brother and his family flew to New York to be with the family for Christmas. On Christmas Eve, my mother arrived at my house with a bottle of wine, decorated beautifully, as her gifts always are. She had wrapped the bottle in snowflake paper and attached a snowflake cookie cutter to the top of the bottle.

The next day, Christmas Day, we were all gathering at my mother's house. I decided I'd make a baked Brie. My mom told me she had enough food, but for some reason I felt compelled to make that Brie. I packed up the ingredients—Brie wheel, apricot preserves, walnuts, and pastry dough—and prepared to go. But then I saw my mom's snowflake cookie cutter on the kitchen counter. And a thought occurred to me: *I'm going to have extra dough, so why not cut a snowflake from the dough and put it on top of the Brie to make it festive?*

At my mother's house, I rolled out the dough and cut a snowflake with the cutter. I guess I messed up, because it came out looking like a Jewish star. I was delighted!

"Look at this!" I called out to my brother and sister. "We have a Jewish-star baked Brie for Christmas!"

I took the dough that was left and rolled it into a long strip to make a circle border for the Brie. I noticed my brother watching me intently.

"What are you doing with that strip of dough?" he asked, almost accusingly.

"I'm making a circle around the star," I said. "I know it's not that creative, but I just felt like doing it. Here, look."

My brother shook his head and walked out of the kitchen.

A moment later, he called me from another room. "Laura, can I see you for a second?" His tone was urgent, almost demanding.

"Coming!" I said.

When I got to him, dough still on my hands, John tried to speak, but he just burst into tears.

"What's wrong, what's wrong?" I asked.

"When Boo crossed, I told her if this is real, if the Other Side is real, she had to send me a sign," he said. "And I told her it had to come from you. The sign I asked for," he sobbed, choking out the words, "was a star with a circle around it."

Now we were both crying.

I realized that if I'd just told John I felt Boo Radley around us, he wouldn't have believed me. The Other Side knew that, too. So the Other Side maneuvered to make Boo's sign happen. They got me to create something, and even gave our mom a hand in it, too. John gave Boo quite an assignment, but she pulled it off! What a Christmas present for John!

I asked my brother, "So now do you finally believe?"

My beautiful brother, the lifelong skeptic, thought for a moment.

"I kind of have to," he said.

We are all capable of recognizing these amazing links to the Other Side. We are all connected to those we love, both here and on the other side. Beyond these connections, I believe we all possess the ability to connect to the Other Side. Maybe we all can't find lost ballet slippers, but who knows—maybe we can.

For my children, I do just as I do for my students, and just as I do for the people I read for, and just as I hope I've done for those who read this book: I encourage them to open their minds and their hearts to the idea that the universe is a bigger and more magical place than we can imagine.

It's the same thing I say to myself every day. I have come to embrace life this way.

Now here is the beautiful part—nothing about our lives has to change, except for our perception.

We all have psychic experiences in our lives that connect us to one another and to those we love on the Other Side. Not just once in a while, but all the time. My wish is that we realize and celebrate the gift we have inside us, and that we come to understand how opening our minds and hearts to it can fundamentally transform our lives.

There won't be any bolts of lightning or claps of thunder. All that will happen is that we'll start to look at our lives differently. But that tiny shift can change your life. It can change the world. It can rattle the universe. And the light between us all will shine even brighter.

ACKNOWLEDGMENTS

This book exists thanks to the light and influence of so many people, in this world and on the Other Side.

Alex Tresniowski—You have been part of this book's journey from the first day of the download. Within twenty-four hours, you appeared to help sculpt it and bring it into the world. I couldn't have asked for a better collaborator. Thank you for all the light you have given. You are one of the most humble people I have ever met and a gift to the world.

Jennifer Rudolph Walsh—You are a life changer and light bringer, not to mention the most supportive and amazing agent—and friend. Your vision and passion are unstoppable and dazzling. Whatever great force of light put me in your path, I am forever grateful. You inspire me and help me to stay grounded. Quite simply, you change the world. So thankful to be on this journey with you and be in your light! Shine on!

Julie Grau—I know that you were handpicked by the Other Side to be the editor of this book and are part of the team of light. Your insight, intelligence, and vision have meant everything to this book's journey; thank you for guiding it home. Thank you for your patience, kindness, and friendship. I know how lucky I am to cross paths with you and I am so grateful.

Linda Osvald, my mom—My first and greatest teacher, you taught me to love, work hard, give to others, be kind, and always follow my heart. You are a great force of love in the world, and you have made all the difference in my life. You made the landscape of my childhood beyond beautiful. And every moment, every sacrifice, every time you cheered me on, told me I was strong and beautiful, believed in me, inspired me, and unconditionally loved me—it all mattered; my path of light was forged by your love. This book is as much a reflection of you as it is me. Whatever I did in a past life to get you as my mom in this one, I am forever thankful. I hit the mom jackpot.

John Osvald, Dad—For all the nights singing in the basement and all the ways you've tried, thank you. I love you.

Marianna Entrup, TT—For always being there, whether it was rescuing us at Brant Lake or dispensing medical advice, you have been part of our family. I love you.

Ann Wood—Thank you for all the kindness and love you have always shown me. You are one classy lady.

Christine Osvald-Mruz—I was born into a world of love as your sister. Thank you for all of our childhood adventures; some of the happiest memories my heart holds are of the times spent with you. You have always been an incredible role model and inspiration. I am blessed and grateful to have such a kind, intelligent, compassionate sister and friend.

John William Osvald—You are one of the most loving, magnanimous, positive-risk-taking, and compassionate people I have ever met—not to mention the best cook I know. The fact that I have you as my brother *and* friend is one of my life's greatest blessings. You inspire me and help me to grow and change in countless ways. The day you were born was one of the happiest days of my life. My soul must have known. . . .

Garrett Jackson—So many of the beautiful, light-filled things that have appeared in my life are because of you. Your heart and my heart, it seems, are old friends—and finding you has been one of my life's greatest treasures. The life we have built is all I dreamed of and more. You challenge me and inspire me and have helped me to grow in immeasurable ways. You are a man of great character, and it is an honor journeying through life—and parenthood—and everything in between with you. I love you so very much.

Ashley Jackson—My firstborn, light-filled daughter. You made me a mom and changed my world forever, infusing it with more love than I ever thought possible. Your beauty, intelligence, artistic ability, and light shine into even the darkest corners of my life.

Hayden Jackson—My sweet Bubba who is so much like me it is scary. You arrived in this world with your shining crown of hair and filled my world with even more love. You teach me new things every day—whether it is about science and gene splicing, or the language and depth of my heart, I am so blessed to be your mom—and so grateful you chose me.

Juliet Jackson—You are bottled sunshine in human form—you bring light, joy, and love wherever you go. Your kind heart and zest for life inspire me and remind me to live life fully and with passion. You are a gift to all who know you—but most of all to me. I am so grateful that I get to be your mom.

Laura Schroff—The invisible thread that drew us together was certainly part of the Other Side's plan. The role you have played in helping this book come to light is immeasurable. You are a great force of light in the world, and I am privileged to not only bask in your glow but to call you a great friend. Thank you for your unending guidance and love on this journey. You inspire me.

Gina Centrello and Gail Rebuck—For believing in the power of this story from the start—and giving it lift. I am certain you are part of the team of light.

Stephanie Nelson—I definitely used my abilities a decade and a half ago when we first met and I told you, a student teacher at the time, that you would need to accept the permanent position at the high school so that you could be my best friend and we could work together. A truer friend I couldn't ask for. Thank you for being there through thick and thin—and for being a fixed light in my world and heart. And how nice of the Universe to make our husbands friends, too! Thankful for Christopher Nelson as well!

Dorene Bair—You are a change agent and connector of everything good in my life! Your bubbly, positive energy is contagious, and I love being around the light of you. Thank you for being an incredible, supportive friend. Everything you do you do with grace, class, and kindness. You inspire me in a myriad of ways! You sparkle. And to your wonderful husband, Tom Bair: thank you for the incredible role you played in helping this book find its place in the world!

Gwen Jordan—Ever since eighth grade, you have been there for countless adventures, phone calls, and escapades; our friendship has been a constant through changes and decades. I am so thankful for the gift of you and look forward to more adventures to come. Thanks for being such a great bestie.

Marris Goldberg—Being around you or even just talking to you always is uplifting. You live life with passion and joy and inspire all those around you. Thank you for being such a shining light in my world and such an incredible friend.

Danielle Lash—Through escapades abroad and adventures here, you always bring the fun and laughter. You are a gift to the world, lighting it up wherever you go. Pish, I'm so grateful for your friendship and presence in my world.

Rachel Rosenberg—Some friends you just know will be forever friends. You are one of those.

Danielle Hain—Tiny, so lucky to have your positive energy in my world! You shine!

Jennifer Schulefand—My former roomie and housemate, so glad to still be connected after so many years.

Drew Katz—While I wish we could have met under different circumstances, I am grateful that the Other Side connected us. You are a person of character, generosity, and strength of spirit—and I know that your dad and mom are very proud of the man that you are.

You embrace the world with kindness and compassion. I feel as if I have known your soul a long time—and am so happy to be in the light of your friendship. My love and gratitude to both you and your wonderful wife, Rachel, always.

Litany Burns and Ron Elgas—Thank you for helping me to see and understand my path and for all the light you put into the world.

Bob and Phran Ginsberg—So much of the work I do in the world is tied to you. You are two of the most giving, inspiring, generous people I have ever met. The work you do in the world helping others, healing grief, and furthering the Other Side's message is immeasurable. I know you are part of the incredible team of light. I cannot fail to thank and mention your daughter Bailey, who has been behind this all along—and is the one who I am sure brought me to your doorstep. What a force of light you all are.

Dr. Julie Beischel—Your commitment to exploring afterlife science means more to our world than you can even fathom. I am so thankful for the role you and Windbridge have played in my life.

John Audette—Your faith and commitment to light work is incredible. I know the Other Side works with you and through you in order to get their message of love and continuation of consciousness out to the world. You are part of a great team of light. Your friendship has been invaluable to me on my journey. Thanks for helping to light the way.

Eben Alexander—Your willingness to share your story with the world is inspiring. Thank you for all you have taught us. I am proud to consider you a friend.

Dr. Mark Epstein—Crossing paths with you has been a great gift. I am so honored to be connected to you. Your light heals and inspires our world.

Dr. Brian Weiss—You light the way for so many here, helping us all understand that our greatest gift is our gift to love and that we are eternal beings. You inspire me in so many ways. Thank you for helping to light the way on my journey.

Dr. Gary Schwartz—Your commitment to exploring and helping others understand the powerful messages the Other Side has to share is inspiring. I am so happy for all the synchronicities and ways our paths have crossed. You have been an important part of my journey, and I honor the light between us.

Teachers play a pivotal role in lighting the way for us all. To all my many teachers, I am thankful—but especially to the following, who helped me see and understand my connection to others, harness the light, and believe in myself: my third-grade teacher, Mrs. Nolan; my fourth-grade teacher, Mrs. Margaret McMorrow; my twelfth-grade English teacher, Mr. Kevin Dineen; and my college English professor, the late Mr. David Bosnick. Thank you doesn't seem adequate. I honor and see the light between us. You are each a part of me and in my heart, always.

Michelle Goldstein—A teacher who has impacted the lives of my children. What an incredible person you are!

Dr. Jane Modoono Philport—You arrived at Herricks High School and immediately gave off a great light. I have learned so much from you. I am grateful for your support, encouragement, love, and friendship. I wish every teacher could have a principal like you. You create greatness wherever you go.

Nicole Cestari Clark—I am thankful the universe connected me to such an amazing woman and friend. Your energy and passion are contagious, and the work you do in the world is filled with light. Anyone who knows you and calls you a friend is lucky.

Laura Castillo—I am so grateful to you for being the most amazing, nurturing, fun babysitter to my kids and the go-to person in my life. There is so much light about you!

Henry Bastos—Thanks for the beauty and friendship you bring to my life.

Lisa Capparelli—Love your energy and love our dinners. Thank you for the gift of your friendship. There is never a dull moment with Dave around, and I look forward to our future escapades!

Paul and Pam Cain—You are a couple who are so filled with light!

Everything you do in this world is touched by your compassion and kindness. I am proud to know you.

Trina and Adam Venit—Love that my path led me to meet two such incredible people! Keep shining your beautiful light!

Starr Porter—What starlight you give off into the world! I am so fortunate to have crossed paths with you—and Chris Wagner—and be connected by cords of light.

Sky Ferreira—You have created a path of light through the dark. I know your team on the Other Side is proud as you continue to share your artistic gifts with the world. I will always be rooting for you—and am honored by your friendship.

To all my nieces, nephews, in-laws, and extended family: Each of you brings beautiful light to the world—and I am so thankful that I get to walk this path with you as family: John, Matt, Willy, Henry, and Peter Mruz, John and Laurie Mruz, Cyndi and Alan Switzer, Natasha Khokhar, Maya, Zoey, and John Osvald, Aliya and Priya Khokhar, Anika Bashir, Angela and Angela G. F. Jackson, Jimmy, Kerry, Joey, Brian, Kevin, and Danny Jackson, John, Emily, Jay, and Johnny Jackson, Lucille Weintraub, Brett, Elyse, Gregg, Karen, Jarrett, and Carol Weintraub, Jimmy, Ted, Maddy, Teddy, and Kenny Wood. And to my loved ones on the Other Side: Omi and Pop Pop, Dundee Yette, Nani and Apa, Vicki; and my in-laws Gary and Alan—you have each played a vital role in my heart and my world. Thank you.

To the extended family of my childhood: Nancy, Lee, Damon, and Derrick Smith, Ellie and Nick Pucciarello—so many happy memories are tied to you.

To all the people who have shared their stories in this book, what a great gift you have given us all. One of the greatest blessings of doing this work is meeting and connecting with incredible people who, in the end, feel more like family than friends. This list includes Susan Newton-Poulter and Fred Poulter, Maria Ingrassia, Kenneth Ring, Nancy Larson, Jim Calzia, RoseAnn DeRupo and Charlie Schwartz, Joe and Maryanne Pierzga, Mary Steffey, Frank McGonagle, and Mike Cestari. And to all the connected family members on the Other Side:

Scotty Poulter, Kyle Larson, Kathy Calzia, Jessie Pierzga, Charlotte, Elizabeth, and the others—we honor you and thank you for bringing us all together and sharing your story and light with the world.

Bobbi Allison—One of my soul sisters and a great light in my world. Thank you for your constant and unwavering love and support. May the universe bless you infinitely for all the kindness and light you bring to others.

Dr. Marc Reitman—I am grateful for the incredible role you played on my path. You are a healer and light bringer in this world! I am honored to know you.

Dr. Jeff Tarrant—Thank you for looking at my brain, finding me some answers, and being a wonderful friend! Your zest for life can be felt by anyone who gets to be around your energy—and I am so thankful to count myself as one of those people.

Amy Lewin—For being an angel and guide on my path here on earth. I am forever grateful for the role you have played. You are one of my favorite people.

Melissa and Tom Gould—Some of the greatest gifts of this work is meeting such wonderful, incredible people like you. I am blessed to know you and call you friends.

Angie Walker, Danielle Perretty, Lynne Ruane, Laura Swan, Rainey Stundis, and Anthony and Grace Avellino—The best part of this work is meeting incredible people who become beautiful friends—I count you among them.

Bill, Angela, and B.J. Artuso—For your commitment to exploring the Other Side and the light of your friendship. I am so happy our paths crossed.

To the rest of my psychic girlfriend crew—What would I do without you? You keep me grounded and keep me laughing. It's so wonderful whenever I am with you: Kim Russo, Janet Mayer, Bethe Altman, Diana Cinquemani, Pat Longo, and the rest of the crew.

And to my first class of psychic and spiritual development students—I could not have asked for a better group of people to explore our connection to one another and the Other Side with!

Thank you for making Wednesday nights shining points of light in my week: Amanda Muldowney, Janine Martorano, Amy Lederer, Marilyn Pilo, Mary Kennedy , Lisa Johnson, Cathleen Costello, Rosemary McNamara, and Linda Pawlak.

To Laura Van der Veer, Katie Giarla, and Maggie Shapiro—Thank you for all the help you provided in helping to bring this book to light and for answering any and all technical questions I had related to it at any time of day or night!

To my team of light at Random House: Sally Marvin, Nicole Morano, Theresa Zoro, Sanyu Dillon, Leigh Marchant, Andrea DeWerd, Greg Mollica, and Nancy Delia ... thank you for taking such good care of me and my work. And to the team at Arrow in the UK: My thanks to Susan Sandon, Jenny Geras, Gillian Holmes, and Jess Gulliver.

To the rest of my team of light at WME, Rafaella De Angelis, Alicia Gordon, Kathleen Nishimoto, and Scott Wachs, so grateful for all you do and the role you've played.

A huge thank-you to the Herricks High School faculty and staff, and all my former students (who I am certain taught me more than I ever taught them). Special love goes to the current and former members of the English department—my family away from home: Jane Burstein, Nancy Rajkowski, Barbara Hoffman, Ed Desmond, Steph Nelson, Alan Semerdjian, Jessica Lagnado, Tom Baier, Tom Mattson, Sonia Dainoff, Kelly Scardina, Sarah Kammerdener, Denise Barnard, Lauren Graboski, David Gordon, Mike Imondi, Mike Stein, Karen Meier, and Victor Jaccarino. And also Chris Brogan, Louise O'Hanlon, Claudia Carter, Joanne Asaro, Trish Basile, Jane Morales, Michele Pasquier, Joanie Keegan, Andrew Frisone, Bryan Hodge, Gail Cosgrove, Jane Modoono, Suzanne Faeth, Sharon Morando, Danielle Yoo, Tania DeSimone, Rich Gaines, Caryn Krutcher, Nicole Cestari, and Deirdre Hayes.

To all the wonderful people who have allowed me into their energy to read for them: I am thankful for each experience and connection.

To the team of light on the Other Side—none of this would be possible or exist without you. Thank you for allowing me to be the messenger and be part of your great light.

And to you, the reader, I am grateful to be on this journey of light together.